EDITIONS

ARMENIAN
BATAK/INDONESIAN
BRITISH SIGN
BULGARIAN
BURMESE (Myanmar)
CATALAN
CHINESE
ENGLISH
  Africa
  Australia
  Chinese/English
  India
  Indonesia
  Japan
  Korean/English
  Korean/English/
   Japanese
  Myanmar
  Philippines
  Sri Lanka
  United Kingdom
  United States
ESTONIAN
FRENCH
GREEK
GUJARATI
HINDI
HUNGARIAN
IBAN/ENGLISH
ILOKANO
INDONESIAN
ITALIAN
JAPANESE
KANNADA
KISWAHILI
KOREAN
MALAYALAM
NEPALI
NORWEGIAN
ODIA
POLISH
PORTUGUESE
  Africa
  Brazil
  Portugal
RUSSIAN
SINHALA
SPANISH
  Caribbean
  Mexico
  South America
  United States
SWEDISH
TAGALOG
TAMIL
TELUGU
THAI
URDU

KT-399-079

THE UPPER ROOM.

WHERE THE WORLD MEETS TO PRAY

Daniele Och
UK editor

INVITATIONAL

INTERDENOMINATIONAL

INTERNATIONAL

37 LANGUAGES
Multiple formats are available in some languages

15 The Chambers, Vineyard
Abingdon OX14 3FE
brf.org.uk

Bible Reading Fellowship (BRF) is a charity (233280)
and company limited by guarantee (301324),
registered in England and Wales

ISBN 978 1 80039 139 0
All rights reserved

Originally published in the USA by The Upper Room® **upperroom.org**
US edition © 2022 The Upper Room, Nashville, TN (USA). All rights reserved.
This edition © Bible Reading Fellowship 2022
Cover image © iStock.com/marchello74

Acknowledgements

Scripture quotations marked with the following abbreviations are taken from the
version shown. Where no acronym is given, the quotation is taken from the same
version as the headline reference.

NRSV: The New Revised Standard Version of the Bible, Anglicised Edition, copyright
© 1989, 1995 by the Division of Christian Education of the National Council of the
Churches of Christ in the USA. Used by permission. All rights reserved.

NIV: The Holy Bible, New International Version (Anglicised edition) copyright © 1979,
1984, 2011 by Biblica. Used by permission of Hodder & Stoughton Publishers, an
Hachette UK company. All rights reserved. 'NIV' is a registered trademark of Biblica.
UK trademark number 1448790.

CEB: copyright © 2011 by Common English Bible.

KJV: the Authorised Version of the Bible (The King James Bible), the rights in which
are vested in the Crown, are reproduced by permission of the Crown's Patentee,
Cambridge University Press.

A catalogue record for this book is available from the British Library

Printed by Gutenberg Press, Tarxien, Malta

How to use *The Upper Room*

The Upper Room is ideal in helping us spend a quiet time with God each day. Each daily entry is based on a passage of scripture and is followed by a meditation and prayer. Each person who contributes a meditation to the magazine seeks to relate their experience of God in a way that will help those who use *The Upper Room* every day.

Here are some guidelines to help you make best use of *The Upper Room*:

1   Read the passage of scripture. It is a good idea to read it more than once, in order to have a fuller understanding of what it is about and what you can learn from it.
2   Read the meditation. How does it relate to your own experience? Can you identify with what the writer has outlined from their own experience or understanding?
3   Pray the written prayer. Think about how you can use it to relate to people you know or situations that need your prayers today.
4   Think about the contributor who has written the meditation. Some users of *The Upper Room* include this person in their prayers for the day.
5   Meditate on the 'Thought for the day' and the 'Prayer focus', perhaps using them again as the focus for prayer or direction for action.

Why is it important to have a daily quiet time? Many people will agree that it is the best way of keeping in touch every day with the God who sustains us and who sends us out to do his will and show his love to the people we encounter each day. Meeting with God in this way reassures us of his presence with us, helps us to discern his will for us and makes us part of his worldwide family of Christian people through our prayers.

I hope that you will be encouraged as you use the magazine regularly as part of your daily devotions, and that God will richly bless you as you read his word and seek to learn more about him.

Daniele Och
UK editor

Volunteer with BRF

At BRF we believe that volunteers have so much to contribute to our work and ministry as we support churches in their mission. We offer numerous opportunities, including the role of local church champion, whereby a volunteer shares the work of BRF with their local church.

Offering such a wealth of ministries for all ages, we are well placed to support churches in a way that is suitable for them and their context. Our volunteers working with church leadership are able to make a difference to the lives of others.

Our team of volunteers includes people from a variety of ages, denominations and backgrounds, each with varying skills. Some have a particular BRF ministry of interest while others are connected across all ministries.

The role is flexible to fit with each person's availability and varies in each setting. Some share information via their church notice sheet or have contact with specific individuals, such as children's or youth leaders or those working with older people. Others have contacts in their Churches Together network or denominational structures. Being well supported by BRF offers an opportunity to feel connected, as well as getting to know others in a similar role.

Angela in Wiltshire volunteered with the encouragement of her rector to encourage individuals and groups to get closer to God through regular study by highlighting the various BRF resources and updates in the parish newsletter.

Catriona Foster, one of BRF's volunteers, says:

I would sum up my volunteering with BRF as a rewarding and inspiring privilege. Not only is volunteering rewarding and enjoyable but recent research has shown that well-being is significantly improved when people are meeting and helping others and feel valued.

As volunteer Martyn Payne so helpfully expresses:

It is when we reach out to help others that we are most helped. This is the surprising equation of giving and receiving that lies at the heart of our faith in God.

If you or someone you know would be interested in joining the team, please contact **jane.butcher@brf.org.uk**

One

The Lord will become king over all the earth; on that day the Lord will be one and his name one.
Zechariah 14:9 (NRSV)

Zechariah 14:9 makes a clear statement of devotion and faith despite the post-exilic chaos from which it emerges. It evokes an image of steadfast hope for the future of Jerusalem as she looks to rise triumphantly from the ashes of her former glory. The prophet Zechariah boldly declares that in the end God's ultimate rule over the nations and God's divine personhood are undiminished, despite apparent evidence to the contrary.

The Hebrew word *echad*, here translated as 'one', means unity, uniqueness, wholeness and indivisibility. This concept is also a pillar of the foundational Shema prayer found in Deuteronomy 6:4–9; 11:13–21 and Numbers 15:37–41. Why is this 'oneness' key to God's identity, and why is it important for us to understand? Simply put, God's essential unity asserted in prophecy and prayer offers us an invitation to a secure relationship with our creator as we navigate our fragmented world. May we by faith dare to proclaim – as Zechariah did – that no matter the circumstances, we will keep our eyes open for God's unwavering love and grace. May that love and grace take root in our governments, neighbourhoods, ministries and families – even as destructive and divisive elements seek to sow chaos among us. God is able.

Revd Kimberly Orr
World editor and publisher

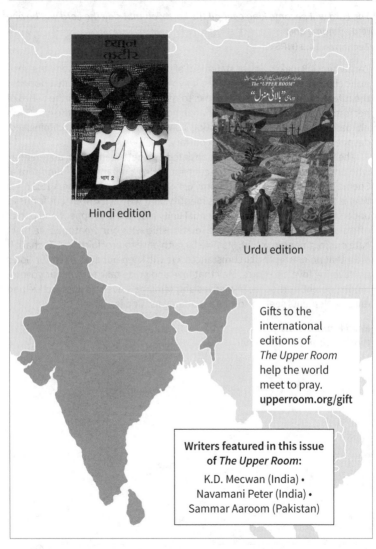

Hindi edition

Urdu edition

Gifts to the international editions of *The Upper Room* help the world meet to pray. **upperroom.org/gift**

Writers featured in this issue of *The Upper Room*:

K.D. Mecwan (India) •
Navamani Peter (India) •
Sammar Aaroom (Pakistan)

The editor writes...

The Lord God made all kinds of trees grow out of the ground – trees that were pleasing to the eye and good for food. In the middle of the garden were the tree of life and the tree of the knowledge of good and evil.
Genesis 2:9 (NIV)

The first thing we are told about God in the Bible is that God is the Creator – 'In the beginning God created the heavens and the earth' (Genesis 1:1). It is not surprising, therefore, that in each issue of *The Upper Room*, several meditations draw upon creation, especially plants and animals, for lessons about what God is like. Jesus himself frequently did this (e.g. Matthew 6:26–29), and both the Old and New Testaments attest to how creation highlights the glory of God (e.g. Psalm 19:1; Romans 1:20).

In this issue of *The Upper Room* you will find many examples of such reflections, and I was struck in particular by the number of references to trees (see especially 12 September and 19 and 25 October).

It is said that apart from God and people, trees are the most mentioned living thing in the Bible. I have not counted that myself, but regardless of the frequency of their mention, trees do feature at key stages in the biblical story. The mysterious trees of 'life' and of 'the knowledge of good and evil' are central to the stories of creation and the fall (Genesis 2—3). The tree of life features again in John's vision of the New Jerusalem (Revelation 22). And at the climax of the biblical story, the cross upon which Jesus is crucified can be seen as a kind of tree (see Galatians 3:13, NRSV). Those are just a few of many examples.

As you may have seen in the back page of each issue of *The Upper Room,* the tree is also a symbol of the work of BRF. The seed of daily Bible reading planted in 1922 has, 100 years later, grown and branched out to various ministries that have touched millions of lives. As you daily meditate on the word of God, with the help of *The Upper Room* community, may you too, in the words of the psalmist, be 'like a tree planted by streams of water, which yields its fruit in season and whose leaf does not wither' (Psalm 1:3).

Daniele Och
UK editor

To explore more on the theme of trees in scripture, check out Martin and Margot Hodson's meditations on 'The wisdom of trees' in *Green Reflections*, available at **brfonline.org.uk**

Shaking the foundations

Read Romans 8:31–39
In all these things we are more than conquerors through him who loved us.
Romans 8:37 (NIV)

In 2011 my best friend from university was killed in a bomb attack in Jerusalem while she was on her way to meet me. She was a Bible translator doing a course in Hebrew. I was a vicar on a pilgrimage to the Holy Land. Being rarely on the same continent, naturally we seized the chance to meet.

That tragedy shook the foundations of my faith. It still affects me and many others who knew her. How could God still be in control of our lives when such random violence could tear everything apart? I grew up in Northern Ireland during the Troubles, yet this was the first time political violence had ever touched anyone close to me. My friend's life and work for God's kingdom were cut off so senselessly. How could God allow it?

The words of Romans 8:31–39, which touched us when we came to faith at university, were the core of the sermon I preached at her funeral, and they remain key to my holding on to God in trust, even without understanding.

The global pandemic of recent years has shaken the foundations of so much in our world, our daily lives and perhaps our faith. But God promises that nothing can separate us from his love in Christ Jesus. When we can't hold on to him, may he give us trust that he holds on to us, always.

Prayer: *Lord, when our foundations are shaken, give us the power to hold on to you in faith, through Christ who loves us. Amen*

Thought for the day: 'God has said, "Never will I leave you; never will I forsake you"' (Hebrews 13:5).

Mercia Flanagan (Northern Ireland, United Kingdom)

Anxiety and faith

Read Psalm 9:9–20
The Lord is a refuge for the oppressed, a stronghold in times of trouble.
Psalm 9:9 (NIV)

I've dealt with anxiety and depression for a long time. Some days I feel like I can take on anything that comes my way; other days I feel like crawling under a rock. The constant stress of the pandemic has turned up the volume on these emotions. Most days, I feel trapped in a bubble with no way to break out.

The stress of these times wears on me, but it has also taught me about God's power, comfort and strength in new ways. I've always been a believer and talk to God on a regular basis, but this year has been different. I've clung to my faith like never before, praying and praising God for each new day and each new blessing. Even though my anxiety still remains, my relationship with my creator helps me to feel calmer and gives me the capacity to think about others. Because God is with me, I can set aside the bad feelings and work for good. And I always remember that it's okay to ask God and others for help.

Prayer: *Dear God, give us strength, guidance and perseverance so we can take on life's challenges and love others like Jesus does. Amen*

Thought for the day: On my darkest days, God's light is still with me.

Derrick Zurn (Pennsylvania, USA)

The best place

Read John 14:1–4

*Do I have anyone else in heaven? There's nothing on earth I desire
except you.*
Psalm 73:25 (CEB)

After our father died following a prolonged illness, my siblings and I tried
to care for our mother by renovating her house and making travel plans
for her to see friends and family. She was excited to have her roof fixed,
create a small garden and spend time with loved ones. Then, suddenly,
she died in her sleep.

Her passing was incredibly painful for us, not only because it was
unexpected but also because we had lost our father so recently. Whereas
our father's illness allowed us some time to prepare for his death, we did
not expect our mother to pass away so soon after. The reality of losing
both parents seemed unbearable.

The morning after her interment, I was filled with sadness. Hoping to
find encouragement, I turned to the Bible and saw Psalm 73:25. I took
that verse as a heaven-sent message for me. It was as if my mother was
assuring me that she was in the best place possible – with God in heaven.
While we get a taste of God's goodness on earth, everything will finally
be made right in the afterlife (John 14:1–4). I miss my parents, but the
thought of their rejoicing in the presence of God eases my pain.

Prayer: *Dear Lord, when we are faced with death, help us to hold on
to the hope of heaven, where we will join the communion of saints
and rejoice in your presence. Amen*

Thought for the day: My joy will be made complete in heaven.

Marlene Legaspi-Munar (Batangas, Philippines)

Keep focused

Read Matthew 14:22–31

But when [Peter] noticed the strong wind, he became frightened, and beginning to sink, he cried out, 'Lord, save me!' Jesus immediately reached out his hand and caught him, saying to him, 'You of little faith, why did you doubt?'
Matthew 14:30–31 (NRSV)

I have led seven trips to Israel over the past 25 years. During the course of those trips, we always take a boat ride on the Sea of Galilee. When we reach the middle, I ask the captain to turn the boat engines off. As we drift along in the water, I read two passages of scripture aloud: Jesus calming the storm (Luke 8:22–25) and Peter walking on the water (Matthew 14:22–23).

On my most recent trip, a small squall began to kick up the waves while we were travelling across the water. It occurred to me that Peter might have seen similar waves and felt a similar wind. And when he took his eyes off Jesus to look at the storm around him, he became fearful and began to sink.

I think we all can relate to Peter when we feel like life is out of our control. But if we turn our focus to Jesus through scripture and prayer, he will always be there to reach out his hand and pull us to safety.

Prayer: *Thank you, Jesus, for your constant presence. Teach us to rely on you in every situation. Amen*

Thought for the day: How will I keep my life focused on Christ today?

Gregory N. Seltzer (Florida, USA)

The power of water

Read John 4:1–15

'Whoever believes in me, as scripture has said, rivers of living water will flow from within them.'
John 7:38 (NIV)

On a recent trip with friends to a nearby lake, I visited a beautiful waterfall. I was able to hear it even before I could see the falling water plunging into the lake below. We anchored our boat and began to swim towards the waterfall. The force of the water, the sound and the coolness didn't scare me. I swam with confidence to the waterfall, letting the water hit me on the head, neck and shoulders. My friends were smiling, and we stayed near the waterfall for quite some time, allowing the cool water to refresh us in the heat of the day.

That majestic waterfall reminded me of God's love, power and constant presence. Jesus offers us living water. He quenches our thirst and fills us with his love until it overflows from us to others. This water satisfies like no other and fills the soul.

Prayer: *Heavenly Father, we want to be filled with your living water so that we may be refreshed and share your love with others. We pray as Jesus taught us, 'Our Father which art in heaven, hallowed be thy name. Thy kingdom come, thy will be done in earth, as it is in heaven. Give us this day our daily bread. And forgive us our debts, as we forgive our debtors. And lead us not into temptation, but deliver us from evil: for thine is the kingdom, and the power, and the glory, forever. Amen.'**

Thought for the day: What evidence of God's love and power do I see in my life?

Susan G. Walters (Kentucky, USA)

PRAYER FOCUS: GRATITUDE FOR GOD'S GIFT OF NATURE
*Matthew 6:9–13 (KJV)

Trusting God

Read 1 Peter 5:6–11

Cast all your anxiety on [God], because he cares for you.
1 Peter 5:7 (NRSV)

In high school, French was a difficult subject for me. I had little interest in it, and my teacher's explanations were unclear to me; so I had difficulty in the course and received bad grades. Full of anxiety, I developed a hatred for the subject and prayed to God that I would never have to study it again.

When I was admitted to university, I learned that I was required to take multiple French courses. Fear gripped me, and I wondered how I would pass the classes. I prayed about my fears and asked God to make a way for me. I had full confidence that God would answer me.

After I had prayed, the Lord gave me courage and inspired in me an unexpected interest in French. I had an excellent French professor and received support from people around me. This, along with my constant trust in God, made learning easy. I excelled in my French courses and exams, and I even became a teaching assistant. It was a wonderful experience!

When we have problems or burdens and don't know what to do, we can turn to God. When we lay our cares upon the Lord in prayer, God has promised to sustain us.

Prayer: *Dear God, strengthen us when we are afraid, and give us confidence to face the challenges before us. Amen*

Thought for the day: God helps me carry my burdens.

Asamoah Joseph Omono (Greater Accra, Ghana)

Spiritual friendship

Read Ephesians 5:19–21

'Where two or three gather in my name, there am I with them.'
Matthew 18:20 (NIV)

In 2009, my friend Michelle and I had the opportunity to attend a Walk to Emmaus spiritual retreat. The experience was filled with community-building, worship and Bible study. We did not want to lose our excitement about our faith when we returned home, so Michelle and I started to meet once a week. We studied different materials and books over a cup of coffee and breakfast.

Eight years after we began our weekly ritual, Michelle moved across the country. I worried that this would make it difficult to continue our special friendship. I had always interpreted Matthew 18:20 as Jesus asking us to meet in person when we study and worship. But meeting virtually with Michelle has taught me that you do not have to be in the same room for the Lord to be with you. All you have to do is join your hearts and minds together.

While we can no longer share a meal at the same table, we continue to share details of our lives and encourage each other in our faith journeys by discussing *The Upper Room*, hymns and books. Our relationship is one that I cherish.

Prayer: *Dear Lord, thank you for the gift of spiritual friendships. For those of us with this type of friendship, bless these relationships. For those of us longing for a friend, please put the right people in our life. Amen*

Thought for the day: My faith is strengthened by the faith of others.

Yvette War Bonnet (Washington, USA)

In times of need

Read Genesis 22:1–14

Abraham called that place 'The Lord will provide'; as it is said to this day, 'On the mount of the Lord it shall be provided.'
Genesis 22:14 (NRSV)

After losing my job due to changes in the economy, I worried about how I would be able to afford essentials like rent and food to feed my significant other and myself. So many thoughts came crashing in on me at once that I began to panic. I told myself to take a deep breath and know that God will provide, just as Abraham told his son in Genesis 22:8.

The next day my doorbell rang. It was my landlord bringing fresh produce in abundance – carrots, onions, garlic, peppers and more. She told me that her friend owned a restaurant that had lots of leftover food. She couldn't bear to see it all go to waste, so she wanted to share her portion of the food with me. My heart was filled with gratitude. My landlord cared enough to offer me the food, but also God was gracious and blessed me through the restaurant owner who didn't even know me. Nothing is too big for God, who uses unexpected situations to provide for our needs.

Prayer: *Dear God, even when we don't know how things will work out, help us to trust that you care for us and will provide for our needs. Amen*

Thought for the day: Even when my future is unclear, God cares for me.

Eileen Nuñez (New Jersey, USA)

Surrender

Read James 4:13–17
Do not be anxious about anything, but in every situation, by prayer and petition, with thanksgiving, present your requests to God.
Philippians 4:6 (NIV)

Long before our children were born, my wife and I started to make plans for their lives. These expectations, hopes and fears seem to be a big part of parenting. We have wondered: *Will our children be good students and professionals? Are they going to keep loving God? Will the world be hard on them?* Sometimes we worry more than pray for them, forgetting that we are all children of the same creator.

For instance, my wife and I were anxious about our daughter's future plans as she neared high school graduation. We envisioned her going to college or doing a short international exchange or working for a year before going back for more schooling. But then Covid-19 spread around the world, and our plans fell apart.

Going to college was not an option and neither was travelling. We turned to God, praying and reading scripture together. The uncertainty of the pandemic has forced us to look to God and remember that the Almighty's love never fails. We find comfort in God's words: 'As the heavens are higher than the earth, so are my ways higher than your ways and my thoughts than your thoughts' (Isaiah 55:9). Our God is all-powerful.

Prayer: *Lord of love and mercy, teach us how to pray and rest in you. Give us our daily bread, and help us to be anxious for nothing. In Jesus' name. Amen*

Thought for the day: I will put my plans in God's hands.

Andre de Albuquerque Caetano (Minas Gerais, Brazil)

Playing our part

Read John 17:20–26

The Lord himself will give you a sign: the virgin will conceive and give birth to a son, and will call him Immanuel.
Isaiah 7:14 (NIV)

From a young age, I was taught at home and in church about God's promises in scripture – those God has already kept and those yet to be fulfilled. I imagine that the childhood of Mary, the mother of Jesus, may have been similar.

In her time, the Jews were eagerly awaiting the Messiah, so they likely studied scriptures that talked about him. Isaiah 7:14 says, 'The virgin will conceive and give birth to a son, and will call him Immanuel.' It amazes me to think that Mary may have sat at the feet of a priest from the temple and heard this passage read, having no idea that it was speaking of her.

Two thousand years later, as you and I read the word of God, we can be assured that we have a part in the unfolding story. We may not have been assigned a role as well-known as Mary's; but when Jesus prayed for future believers in John 17:20–26, he was talking about us. Our part in the story is to be united with other believers so that all will see the love of Christ in us. When we follow God's commands by loving one another, we become important characters in the best story ever written.

Prayer: *Dear God, thank you for allowing us to play a part in your unfolding story. Help us to love others the way Jesus prayed we would and to share your truth every day. Amen*

Thought for the day: I am an important part of God's unfolding story.

Jody Williams (Illinois, USA)

Holding fast

Read 2 Corinthians 4:7–12, 16–18

We know that in all things God works for the good of those who love him, who have been called according to his purpose.
Romans 8:28 (NIV)

As a young child, I was diagnosed with several conditions affecting my eyes, joints and blood vessels. Despite a childhood full of medical appointments and eye surgeries, I eventually lost sight in my right eye. Forty years later, it is by God's grace that I have any vision at all.

Honestly, all that I've gone through sometimes seems a bit senseless, and I don't feel like my faith has been strengthened as a result. I am thankful for God's blessings; but while scripture says we should have patience in suffering (see Romans 12:12), I just want the surgeries and pain to end.

My perspective widened when I joined a prison ministry a year ago. As I nervously shared my story in front of a gymnasium full of women, everyone was silent and I couldn't see any faces. But by the time I reached the end, there were shouts of 'Amen!' and 'Hallelujah!' Women came to hug me afterward with tears in their eyes.

Perhaps when suffering does not refine our own faith it can offer inspiration for others. While I may not feel like my faith has grown because of my health, I have not abandoned it. Rather, I hold on to faith despite my trials. And maybe that's what really matters.

Prayer: *Dear Lord, in spite of our suffering and trials, help us to hold steadfastly on to you. Empower us to share our stories so our vulnerability may be a gift to others. Amen*

Thought for the day: Even when my pain feels senseless, I can share hope through vulnerability.

Christine Adhikari (Georgia, USA)

Simple pleasures

Read Ecclesiastes 9:7–10

Go, eat your food with gladness, and drink your wine with a joyful heart, for God has already approved what you do.
Ecclesiastes 9:7 (NIV)

I enjoy looking at the chirimoya (custard apple) trees in my garden from my patio and watching them grow each day. They are quite plentiful – far too many for one person to eat. The fresher they are, the more delicious and aromatic the fruit. When I pick the chirimoyas, I already have in mind the people I will be giving them to.

This morning, though, I saw a large, ripe chirimoya I had missed during my earlier picking. I thought, *If someone doesn't eat it soon, it will go to waste.* On the horizon, the sun was just beginning to peek through. I looked at the sky as I took in the panorama and felt God was offering the fruit to me. I sat down in my garden, facing the morning sun and enjoyed its warmth on my face. I started eating slowly, savouring the fruit. I thought about the many blessings in my life. Filled with God's love and goodness, I quietly repeated today's verse from Ecclesiastes: 'Go, eat your food with gladness.' A simple pleasure. I have never enjoyed a chirimoya more.

Prayer: *Creator God, source of all life and goodness, you bring us the gifts of joy and peace. Greater still are the gifts of your love and presence. Thank you, Lord! Amen*

Thought for the day: God is good and generous.

Juan Guerrero (Valle del Cauca, Colombia)

United through prayer

Read Romans 15:1–6
The body is not made up of one part but of many.
1 Corinthians 12:14 (NIV)

I began my first teaching position at Fort Knox, Kentucky, as an English instructor for military recruits predominately from Puerto Rico and South Korea. We focused not only on English skills, but also on the practical understanding of military terminology and materials.

A few of my students were married with children, and one infantry soldier would soon report to his first duty station. On the morning of 5 March 1982, I mentioned to my students that it happened to be the World Day of Prayer. One student spoke up, 'Hey, Teacher, sounds like you want to say a prayer.' So we formed a circle and bowed our heads. I prayed for each of them to return safely to their families. As I finished, another student prayed in Spanish, followed by another praying in Korean. We each concluded with a resounding 'Amen'. After we raised our heads, the silence and brief glances of understanding sanctified the bond of fellowship among us. United in faith, we could see that the strength of prayer was indeed universal.

Prayer: *Dear God, guard us against all fear, and instil in us the power of faith and hope. Thank you for the gift of community. Amen*

Thought for the day: Prayer unites me with Christians around the world.

Pamela Cheeseman (Kentucky, USA)

Running with Jesus

Read John 11:25–36
'In [God] we live and move and have our being.'
Acts 17:28 (NIV)

I felt numb in the weeks following my 50-year-old brother's death. My daily devotional time devolved into daydreaming. Procrastination replaced time set aside for prayer. Tears came easier than praise.

I was frozen, mourning my brother who spent his life in perpetual motion. He embodied Acts 17:28 by living, moving and being in the presence of the Lord. He began walking at eight months, mastered any sport he attempted, gave full-body bear hugs, kneeled when he prayed and clapped to praise songs. My brother, who used his athleticism and his body to glorify God, was gone. I felt alone and unmoored.

My usual ways of connecting with God felt hollow. Then God led me to take a page from my brother's life in order to cope with his death. I needed to interact with God using my body, mind and spirit. I started a running regimen. Some runs were filled with intercessory prayers for our parents and my brother's children. Some runs were spent peppering God with questions about my brother's too-short life. As I ran, I became aware of my rhythmic footsteps and God's air in my lungs as a healing balm for my spirit.

Mile after mile, I experienced God's presence and understanding. And just as Jesus loved and wept for his friends, he wept with me and gave me peace as we ran the miles together.

Prayer: *Dear Jesus, thank you for loving us and for your promise of life eternal. Amen*

Thought for the day: God is with me every step of my way.

Lea Anne Foster (Virginia, USA)

The importance of unity

Read Ephesians 4:1–13

So we, being many, are one body in Christ, and every one members one of another.
Romans 12:5 (KJV)

Many years ago, my football team was down 3-0 at the end of the first half. As we gathered around the coach for halftime, we blamed one another for the errors that had led the rival team to score. Our coach ignored our complaints and handed a sweeping broom made from a bundle of twigs to our team captain and told him to break it. We all watched with keen interest as this guy whom we all respected tried and tried to break the broom but could not even bend it. He ultimately handed it back intact. Looking around at each of us, our coach explained that this was the power of unity. He encouraged us to work together, and in the second half we played with renewed team spirit, scored five goals and won the game.

I think the Holy Spirit wants to teach us a similar lesson. Ephesians 4:6 reminds us that there is 'one God and Father of all'. God wants all believers to unite as one. We're all children of God. Despite our differences, Christians can and should work together to spread the good news.

Prayer: *Dear Lord, help us to set aside our differences and work with Christians around the world, worshipping, serving and glorifying you. Amen*

Thought for the day: There is one God and Father of all.

Samuel Yali Ituma (Ebonyi, Nigeria)

Quilt of blessings

Read Psalm 105:1–4

When [Barnabas] arrived and saw what the grace of God had done, he was glad and encouraged them all to remain true to the Lord with all their hearts.
Acts 11:23 (NIV)

My dear friend Barb makes quilts out of old T-shirts that carry special memories for their owners. One day while I was visiting her, she showed me a quilt she had made for her son that highlighted his high school sports. When I told her of all the T-shirts that I had saved over the years, she graciously volunteered to make a quilt for me. I was thrilled and gratefully accepted. I finally had a purpose for all the old T-shirts that meant so much to me and held so many memories.

As I gathered the shirts, I realised that they all reminded me of the blessings God had given me throughout my life. I now have the T-shirt quilt on my bed, and what a joy it is! Every evening and morning as I get in or out of my bed, I review the T-shirts and thank God for my many good friends and loving family members who helped me make all those memories. I have found that giving thanks to my heavenly Father is a very gratifying way to mark each day.

Prayer: *Dear heavenly Father, thank you for daily reminders of the blessings you have given us. Thank you for bringing us comfort and showing us your love. Amen*

Thought for the day: Today I thank God for my loved ones and the joys we have shared.

Katherine Turk (Wisconsin, USA)

Through my parents' eyes

Read Exodus 4:10–17

The Lord said to [Moses]… 'Now go; I will help you speak and will teach you what to say.'
Exodus 4:11–12 (NIV)

Both my mum and my dad were deaf most of their lives. Neither was born deaf; they lost their hearing as children because of illness. While both had a disability, they overcame many challenges and obstacles to become happy and loving people. They approached life head on and never let their deafness stand in their way.

While Mum and Dad lacked the ability to hear, they had an extremely strong sense of sight and observation. They could walk into a room, walk back out and then tell you about the room in vivid detail. When they met someone, they could read the person's facial expressions, gestures and non-verbal cues and make accurate statements about that person's disposition or mindset without ever hearing them speak.

God knows and provides what we need. Moses was not a great speaker, but God gave him what he needed to be a leader.

I often think of my parents when I am feeling inadequate or unqualified. What they lacked in hearing, God made up for in other ways. Even in the face of immense challenges, God will provide a way for us.

Prayer: *Heavenly Father, thank you for your gift of grace. You have made each of us unique and will provide us with all that we need when we seek your will for our lives. Amen*

Thought for the day: I will embrace the special gifts God has given me.

Brian Foster (North Carolina, USA)

Strength in weakness

Read Hebrews 4:12–16

I am content with weaknesses, insults, hardships, persecutions and calamities for the sake of Christ; for whenever I am weak, then I am strong.

2 Corinthians 12:10 (NRSV)

In the past I would wake up some mornings with a feeling of dread. I thought about my failures, fears and rejections. I wondered why I hadn't accomplished more by now and why I hadn't fulfilled my dreams. I felt I had not lived up to society's standards. Usually as the day went on, I would forget about these thoughts, but they would return another day.

Then I started incorporating prayer more consistently into my life. Whenever dread started surfacing in the morning, I would begin to pray. I started to realise that what I perceived as weaknesses – my fears, regrets and dislikes – had moulded me into a more humble, empathetic and resilient person. Through prayer I began to recognise my identity and self-worth in Christ. I began to celebrate my small victories and stopped dwelling on my assumed failures.

Most important, I learned never to stop striving to be more like Christ. My weaknesses have proven to me that I am human, but the grace of Christ enables me to change, grow and improve. I believe that times of weakness, pain and suffering can become sources of strength. Now I view my times of struggle as lessons and gifts, and I no longer wake up with dread.

Prayer: *Dear God, thank you for being by our side through the challenges life brings. Amen*

Thought for the day: Prayer can help me discover strength in my weaknesses.

Maria Montemayor (Ontario, Canada)

Hold on

Read Hebrews 3:1–6

Let us hold unswervingly to the hope we profess, for he who promised is faithful.

Hebrews 10:23 (NIV)

It was a beautiful September afternoon, and I was picking the apples from my dad's tree, under his instruction, when the ladder slipped. The apples dropped from my hands as I grabbed the nearest branch to prevent my fall. 'Hold on,' my dad encouraged. 'I'll move the ladder.' I had no intention of doing otherwise!

I waited and waited as my elderly father slowly and carefully positioned the ladder to be within my reach and then secured it with his foot. All I could do was to wait and hold on. Eventually, with aching arms, I was able to descend.

Times of waiting are hard. In doubt, difficulty or despair, we long to do something, but often there is nothing we can do to change the circumstances. We simply have to wait. What we can do, however, as I learnt, is to hold on. We hold on by faith in God. We hold on to his promises. We hold on to what we have already known of God's power, presence, provision, truth and goodness.

Whether or not we have reached the end of our own resources and strength, be encouraged today. Be determined to hold on to God. Discover that he never, ever, lets us go. Discover the depths of his love and care for us.

Prayer: *Father, this day I hold on to all I know of you. May I know you are there for me. Amen*

Thought for the day: I hold on to God and am always held.

Hilary Allen (England, United Kingdom)

Cleansing tears

Read Matthew 5:1–12
Blessed are those who mourn, for they will be comforted.
Matthew 5:4 (NIV)

I sat in a rocking chair on the front porch of our farmhouse watching the rain drench my garden as a storm moved across the cornfields. Almost immediately the air cooled, and the ground soaked up much-needed rain. Even though the rainfall interrupted my outdoor plans, I knew it offered the earth necessary nourishment.

Earlier in the day I was in church singing an old familiar hymn. The words touched the fresh grief in my soul over the recent death of my sister. My tears rushed forth, replacing my repressed anger with renewed hope and cleansing my soul. Though death had claimed my sister, she now rests in the arms of Jesus, healed and whole.

The Bible tells us that the Lord bottles our tears (see Psalm 56:8). The Lord cares for us in our grief and comforts us as we mourn. Someday there will be no need for tears of sorrow as we reunite with our loved ones in heaven. But for now, I want my tears to wash me clean of the bitterness that clings to me as I witness the world's suffering. I hold fast to God's promise to right all these wrongs. Then, one day Jesus will return to cleanse the earth, making everything new – and we'll witness all of God's creation healed and whole once more.

Prayer: *Thank you, Lord, for the rain that nourishes the earth and the tears that cleanse our hearts. Amen*

Thought for the day: Through my tears God opens my heart to healing.

Suzanne Montgomery (Indiana, USA)

The gift

Read Luke 10:38–41

'Martha, Martha,' the Lord answered, 'you are worried and upset about many things, but few things are needed – or indeed only one. Mary has chosen what is better, and it will not be taken away from her.'

Luke 10:41–42 (NIV)

I really enjoy classical music. The Brandenburg Concertos by Bach are special favourites of mine. The history of these pieces makes them even more intriguing. Bach composed them and sent the scores in his own handwriting to the Margrave of Brandenburg-Schwedt in 1721. However, the full score remained untouched in the library until the Margrave's death in 1734, and it was not published until 1850. It's amazing to me that such a beautiful gift was neglected for so long.

This reminds me of the gift of salvation that is available to every one of us. Some never open this gift and so never experience the joy it can bring. The reasons are many and complex. But those who do open the gift find abundant living and receive life eternal with God.

So when I hear the Brandenburg Concertos, I remember the gift of salvation that God offers us through Jesus Christ.

Prayer: *Lord Jesus, thank you for your precious gift of salvation. May we live a life of loving service as our way of showing our gratitude. Amen*

Thought for the day: I can encourage others to accept God's gift of salvation.

Bill Gosling (Western Australia, Australia)

Journey to stability

Read Jeremiah 31:1–6

The Lord appeared to us in the past, saying: 'I have loved you with an everlasting love; I have drawn you with unfailing kindness.'
Jeremiah 31:3 (NIV)

Seventeen years ago, I had a breakthrough and finally understood the Lord's love for me. For decades I had begged God to deliver me from my eating disorders and clinical depression. They were taking a toll on my relationships, and I felt like even God had given up on me. I prayed, 'God, I'm constantly letting people down, including myself. From now on, I'm going to focus on your love for me.'

Something changed when I heard myself speak with certainty of the Lord's love for me. In a powerful way I knew my heavenly Father loved me and was on my side. I knew that God never had and never would give up on me. I no longer felt that God was exasperated with me – I sensed God's tenderness.

That day began my slow and steady progress out of emotional instability. After a lot of counselling, the right medication for a while and, most of all, lots of time with God through prayer and Bible reading, I found stability.

I'm glad I didn't wait until my situation got worse. Even though my situation seemed hopeless, I learned to trust in God's love for me and sought the help I needed.

Prayer: *Lord God, surround us with your compassion and fill us with renewed hope. Amen*

Thought for the day: God's love has the power to deliver me from hopelessness.

Sheryl H. Boldt (Florida, USA)

PRAYER FOCUS: THOSE STRUGGLING WITH EATING DISORDERS

Finding peace

Read Isaiah 66:10–13

This is what the Lord says: 'I will extend peace to her like a river, and the wealth of nations like a flooding stream.'
Isaiah 66:12 (NIV)

Whenever I read Isaiah 66 where the prophet speaks about restoring peace and prosperity to Jerusalem, it reminds me of when our family lived in Berlin during the Cold War. It was a city literally divided by the Berlin Wall. As a result, a certain tension always hung in the air.

One day our family stopped at the ruins of an old castle as we travelled through West Germany. Climbing up to a terrace, I looked down on the Rhine River Valley and experienced a peace that seemed to push away all the concerns in my life. God's Spirit was present, and peace was flowing over me like the river below. Although that was many years ago, I have never forgotten that moment.

With time, I've learned that the peace of the Lord is also available through prayer and meditation on scripture. We can trust the Prince of Peace with all our burdens. He will surround us like a river whenever we seek him and surrender our lives to him.

Prayer: *Dear God, help us to seek your peace every day, in good times and in hard times, as we pray, 'Father, hallowed be your name, your kingdom come. Give us each day our daily bread. Forgive us our sins, for we also forgive everyone who sins against us. And lead us not into temptation.'* Amen*

Thought for the day: What burdens can I give to the Lord today?

John Schliesser (Alabama, USA)

PRAYER FOCUS: THOSE LIVING IN CONSTANT TURMOIL
*Luke 11:2–4

Navigating changes

Read Genesis 1:20–23
Clothe yourself with the new person created according to God's image in justice and true holiness.
Ephesians 4:24 (CEB)

When our daughter was four years old, we received a chrysalis in a clear jar. I explained to her that it was God's plan for a caterpillar to change into a beautiful butterfly. We kept a close watch on it because we could already see the wings inside.

Then one afternoon we saw that the butterfly was halfway out! Hurriedly, we took the jar outside. The butterfly worked its way out and stood on the rim of the jar, wobbling back and forth, hesitating. As it attempted to fly, it kept going up and down, almost hitting the ground. My daughter's hand slid into mine. 'Do something, Mummy!' Suddenly, the butterfly soared up and away.

It struck me how we humans are often like that when we go through a major change – like moving to a new home, school or job. We can feel wobbly and unsure in our efforts to adjust. But if we keep working at it, we eventually settle into our new way of life.

God is an awesome creator who speaks to us through creation. I can look back on my life and recognise times when I was like that butterfly. But with God's help, I made it through difficult seasons of change time and time again.

Prayer: *Mighty God, thank you for your presence with us as we encounter life's ups and downs. Amen*

Thought for the day: Though change may be difficult, God gives me strength to endure.

L. Torpy Skinner (Tennessee, USA)

Always on time

Read Isaiah 55:8–13

Trust in the Lord with all your heart; don't rely on your own intelligence.
Proverbs 3:5 (CEB)

In September 2017 my job contract came to an abrupt end. I was devastated and felt hopeless. *How would I find new employment when companies were wrapping up business for the year? How would my family survive? Who would come to our rescue?* I had no back-up plan, and I thought it would be impossible to find a job in the last quarter of the year.

While I was pondering my next move, I believe God gave me the thought to visit my wife's sister. After staying with her for a couple of days, I felt another prompt to visit a local school I had seen. With my CV in hand, I went to see the principal.

I got the surprise of my life when the principal told me that a business teacher was about to go on maternity leave, so they needed a temporary teacher. I was so relieved! Was it just by chance that I travelled to visit my sister-in-law and went to this school? I think not. When I could not see a way forward, God never left my side. God had made arrangements well in advance for me.

Prayer: *God of all wisdom, teach us to not fret when our plans fall apart. Remind us always to depend on your wisdom. Amen*

Thought for the day: Today I will give thanks for God's providence.

Say Amen (Gauteng, South Africa)

Filled with new peace

Read Psalm 121

I will lift up mine eyes unto the hills, from whence cometh my help. My help cometh from the Lord, which made heaven and earth.
Psalm 121:1–2 (KJV)

In 2007, my 29-year-old son, Deon, was murdered. He was a loving, caring and giving person. The grief I endured was tremendous. For months in my brokenness I cried – consumed with unimaginable pain.

One day, I was sitting quietly, asking God, *Why?* In that moment, I felt God telling me that my hurt could be healed if I would allow it. Finally, the healing process began. I started thanking God for sustaining me and restoring peace deep within me. I also thanked God for having given me my son, for the time we spent together, and the joy we shared during his lifetime.

A few years later, I found myself witnessing to others who had also experienced the loss of a child. I felt even closer to God as a result. I learned true forgiveness and compassion for others as I shared my experience with them. God can redeem acts of evil and the suffering that follows. For me, these encounters with others who are grieving are examples of such divine redemption.

Prayer: *Dear heavenly Father, thank you for your mercy. Thank you for giving us strength during our most trying times. Amen*

Thought for the day: There is nothing God can't redeem.

Florece Graham (North Carolina, USA)

The privilege of prayer

Read James 5:13–16

Jesus told his disciples a parable to show them that they should always pray and not give up.
Luke 18:1 (NIV)

I have recently found myself frustrated with how difficult it is to communicate in today's world. Many medical providers are so busy it takes several weeks or months to see a doctor. And recently, I was trying to fix a billing problem over the phone and was transferred to three different people before I connected with the right person. She didn't seem very happy to be talking to me, but we finally resolved the issue.

Communication is hard, especially with large organisations. This makes me keenly appreciate the privilege of prayer. Interacting with God isn't limited to certain hours. There is no waiting; the Almighty is always available. And when we pray to God, our creator is delighted to hear from us. We know we are talking to the right person because God knows us better than we know ourselves.

God wants us to pray. We see this command all over the Bible. We were created to have a relationship with God, and prayer is the best way we can do that.

Prayer: *Gracious and loving God, thank you for the privilege of allowing us to talk to you – anytime, anywhere. Help us to embrace the gift of prayer so that we can grow closer to you. Amen*

Thought for the day: God is always available.

John D. Bown (Minnesota, USA)

Love everyone

Read John 13:1–17

I have set you an example that you should do as I have done for you.
John 13:15 (NIV)

I can vividly imagine the foot-washing scene in the gospel of John: Jesus taking off his outer garment, wrapping a towel around his waist, kneeling to remove the disciples' sandals, and then washing and drying one dusty foot after another. My eyes well up at the image. If the Saviour of the world was willing to take on such a humble task, we should all be willing to serve others too, regardless of who we are and who they are.

Following Jesus' example of servant leadership means being willing to engage with those around us no matter their background. Because of Jesus' love for us, we can show love to everyone, no matter our similarities or differences. So let us strive to show others a love that says, 'We are more alike than we are different.' A love that respects everyone's right to have differing opinions. A love that asks, 'How can I help you?' A love that acknowledges our own weaknesses and shortcomings. A love that focuses on Jesus.

Prayer: *Heavenly Father, help us to remember your sacrifice for us. Guide us to spread the love and joy of Christ to all we meet. In Jesus' name. Amen*

Thought for the day: Jesus calls me to look beyond earthly divisions and to love all people.

Janis Gregg Pressley (Maryland, USA)

A message from God

Read Mark 5:21–43

'You will call on me and come and pray to me, and I will listen to you.'
Jeremiah 29:12 (NIV)

My husband had been ill for several days, and we were worried he may have contracted the Covid-19 virus. We live with our parents and young children, and the idea of spreading the virus to them troubled us. We had him tested for the virus, and we found it challenging to wait patiently for the results.

Each evening after dinner, my children, their caretaker and I gather to read a passage from a children's Bible. That evening when I opened the Bible to our story for the day, the title was 'Jesus heals'. I flipped back a page thinking maybe I had skipped ahead, but I hadn't. I was filled with heartfelt gratitude because I knew God was speaking to me. I told my children's caretaker about how God speaks to us through scripture. We need only to approach God faithfully, and God will guide us through our trials.

That night as I read aloud the story of Jesus giving life to Jairus' sick daughter, I was assured that whatever test result my husband received, God would lead us through the tribulation. It was a peaceful night.

Prayer: *Dear God, guide our paths as we face everyday trials. Help us not to be anxious but rather assured of your presence and protection. Amen*

Thought for the day: Scripture reminds me that God is always near.

Sammar Aaroom (Punjab, Pakistan)

Last year's lilies

Read Revelation 21:1–5

The one who was seated on the throne said, 'See, I am making all things new.'
Revelation 21:5 (NRSV)

Last week I noticed something in our yard that had escaped my attention for an entire season. In all of my comings and goings from home, I had failed to see several lilies that were on the verge of blooming.

The lilies were from last year's Easter service. My wife and I had brought them home and diligently cared for them. However, instead of discarding the lilies when they died, we planted them near the entryway of our home. Somehow, they survived the cold, hard winter. Then with the spring sun and the rejuvenating showers, last year's lilies bloomed again.

We have all had to bury something in a season of hardship and uncertainty. In doing so, perhaps we yielded to the spirit of loss. But we can all find strength in the fact that God has the power to revive, restore, renew and even resurrect. Indeed, God can turn tragedies into triumphs and what we perceive as failure into freedom. Now even if I do not *see* the beauty of last year's lilies, I cannot escape their delightful fragrance. It is the aroma of God who makes all things new.

Prayer: *Dear God, help us to perceive your power to create and recreate in every season of life. Amen*

Thought for the day: I will trust God's power to make all things new.

Shawn M. Wilson (Maryland, USA)

Never really behind

Read Colossians 3:1–3, 12–17

Let the peace of Christ rule in your hearts, to which indeed you were called in the one body. And be thankful.

Colossians 3:15 (NRSV)

Date nights. New cars. New homes. Engagement rings. Smiling children. It feels like every time I log on to social media, this is all I see, while I'm still single, working on my degree and feeling at times like my life is going nowhere. Though I am genuinely glad for my friends who have reached major life milestones, I can't help but feel that I am lagging behind.

Despite my insecurities, I do have a roof over my head, food to eat, clothes on my back, family and friends who love me, a secure college career and, most important, the love and salvation of Jesus Christ. While the material aspects of life are important to us and to our relationships with one another, even more important is our relationship with God. As we go about our life's journey noting the successes of others, we should remember what we have and be thankful for the gifts God gives us – especially the peace of Christ!

Prayer: *Dear Lord, thank you for all you have given us. Help us to appreciate daily blessings as well as our salvation through the atoning sacrifice of Jesus. Amen*

Thought for the day: The love of God is the source of my peace.

Hannah Fewell (Louisiana, USA)

Wafers with love

Read 1 Corinthians 11:23–26

They devoted themselves to the apostles' teaching and to fellowship, to the breaking of bread and to prayer.
Acts 2:42 (NIV)

I met Eva in 1995 during a meeting of the World Day of Prayer International Committee in Australia. We became friends, and though she lived in Poland and I lived in India, we continued to communicate and pray for each other's families. Eva's family had a tradition of celebrating Holy Communion together on Christmas Eve, and beginning in 1996 she sent wafers to my family so that we could participate in Communion and be in fellowship with her family on Christmas Eve. My husband and I followed this tradition each year.

One year the wafers did not arrive, and I knew in my heart something must have happened. I later came to know through a mutual friend that Eva had passed away. Our nationalities, language, skin colour and traditions were different, but the foundation of our friendship was 'one Lord, one faith, one baptism'. Our Christian fellowship was strengthened by our participation in Holy Communion.

The wafers and wine of Communion remind us of God's amazing grace and sacrifice, connecting people of faith across the world. Praise God that we are part of this fellowship!

Prayer: *Gracious God, we thank you for your redeeming love. Help us to remember this love with gratitude when we participate in Holy Communion. Amen*

Thought for the day: Communion connects me to Christians around the world.

Navamani Peter (Karnataka, India)

Overcoming challenges

Read Psalm 86:1–7

In the day of my trouble I call on you, for you will answer me.
Psalm 86:7 (NRSV)

After a difficult shoulder surgery, I was severely limited in my daily activities and spent many of my days alone. I developed anxiety and, according to my counsellor, a form of PTSD. I was depressed, lost weight and couldn't sleep. I was shaking uncontrollably. I was overwhelmed with negative thoughts. Daily I would call out to God, 'Please help me, God. I can't live like this!'

One afternoon, a voice in my mind said, 'You'll make it.' Just that simple phrase. Soon after, with the proper medications, much prayer, professional counselling and the support of my wonderful wife, I began to recover. I would not wish this experience on anyone. But through all of this, I gained new understanding and concern for mental health issues as well as a better relationship with God. When I learned how to truly open myself to God's Spirit and strength, God really did answer me in my time of need.

Prayer: *Heavenly Father, thank you for your strength and love that sustain us in our daily lives. Amen*

Thought for the day: God truly listens to me in my times of need.

Marty Smith (Pennsylvania, USA)

Neighbours in need

Read Matthew 20:25–28

Serve wholeheartedly, as if you were serving the Lord, not people, because you know that the Lord will reward each one for whatever good they do.
Ephesians 6:7–8 (NIV)

'God, grant me an opportunity to help someone today,' I prayed. It didn't take long to receive an answer. After I returned from the store, I noticed an elderly neighbour struggling to manoeuvre her walker and open the door at the same time. I ran to her assistance, held the building door open and then helped her with her apartment door as well. After receiving her thanks, I returned to my apartment and thanked God for the chance to help a neighbour in need.

We each have opportunities to serve others every day. When we pray for God to direct our steps and open our eyes to ways to serve, our creator is delighted to answer our requests. We can help an elderly person with their groceries or take the time to talk to a lonely friend on the phone. Regardless of how we love others, we can experience a sense of delight when we serve others and glorify God.

Prayer: *Heavenly Father, open our hearts to see opportunities to serve others and learn what it means to love like you today. In Jesus' name. Amen*

Thought for the day: God will grant me an opportunity to help someone today.

Jodi Wheeler (Arizona, USA)

Forget your past mistakes

Read Isaiah 43:16–21

'Forget the former things; do not dwell on the past.'
Isaiah 43:18 (NIV)

A few years after completing my civil engineering degree, I prayed and fasted in the hope that God would provide me with a job with a multinational company. God answered me, and I was offered a wonderful opportunity; but it was not exactly what I had hoped for. Naively, I rejected the position.

As years passed, I began to look back in regret. I realised I had missed a great opportunity in the job I rejected. I began to see myself as a failure because I struggled to secure another job and support my family.

But when I came across this scripture, it spoke to me. I decided to forget my past mistakes and move ahead. I have learned my lessons, so I should move on. I chose to believe God's promise, and this brought a new energy to my life.

When we live in the past, we may miss out on greater things. We can learn from our past mistakes, but we shouldn't dwell on them. Similarly, it is good to be happy about our past achievements, but we shouldn't dwell on them either. God is always making things new, and when we place our trust in Christ, we can hold on to the hope of the beautiful things that are still to come.

Prayer: *Dear God, give us wisdom not to dwell on our past mistakes. Heal our wounds and do a new thing in our lives. In Jesus' name. Amen*

Thought for the day: God is always doing a new thing in my life.

Amobichukwu Samuel Duruaku (Rivers State, Nigeria)

Finding peace

Read Philippians 4:4–9

The peace of God, which surpasses all understanding, will guard your hearts and your minds in Christ Jesus.
Philippians 4:7 (NRSV)

Worrying seemed to come naturally to me. I worried about the past: *Did I say the wrong thing? Make the wrong choice?* And I worried about the future: *Is everything going to work out? Will I do the right thing?* This pattern made it difficult to enjoy life. For years, I searched for ways to change. I found lots of things that helped: yoga, exercise and books on the topic. My doctor prescribed meditation or contemplative prayer. Contemplative prayer is about listening: saying a prayer and then focusing on breathing in and out. This allows us to hear the answers God sends. It might not be words that we hear but rather a feeling of love and comfort.

Through prayer, I have come to know in my heart that God loves me, wants the best for me and is always with me. God takes away my worries and fills me with divine peace and love. In the past I had been concerned that my issues were not big enough to bother God with, but now I know that God loves every person and wants to help all of us.

Now when I start the old pattern of worrying, I try to recognise it and say a prayer. Then I take some deep breaths and wait for the peace of God to fill my mind and heart. While worrying closes me off, feeling connected with God's love opens me up to joyously live my life.

Prayer: *Dear God, take away our worries and fill us with peace. In Jesus' name we pray. Amen*

Thought for the day: In both the big and little concerns of life, God wants to help me.

Jennifer Jennings (Tennessee, USA)

Personal relationships

Read Mark 1:40–45
Immediately the leprosy left him, and he was made clean.
Mark 1:42 (NRSV)

During a mission trip to Jamaica, my high-school group ran sports camps and youth groups all day, shared testimonies in front of large gatherings and did manual labour. But what I most looked forward to each day was visiting patients at a rural infirmary. Seeing the suffering of the patients and the poor condition of the building initially made my heart sink. But there was one man I got to sit with and talk to each day. Eyes lighting up, he would eagerly tell me stories, read me scripture and encourage me and then allow me to do the same for him. Of all the work we were doing in the area, this relationship became the most meaningful for me.

It is easy to forget the importance of nurturing individual relationships. Jesus shows us a better way at the end of Mark 1, when he takes a break from addressing the crowds to heal and interact with one man. The Saviour, God incarnate, came to save the world. He fed the multitudes, but he also healed the man with leprosy and the man with the withered hand. If Jesus had time and found value in connecting with the seemingly forgotten individuals around him, we can do the same.

Prayer: *Dear Lord, open our eyes to the lives of people around us. Give us the courage to reach out to people on a personal level. Amen*

Thought for the day: Today I will make time to share God's love with someone new.

John Keeports (Pennsylvania, USA)

Grow and prosper

Read Psalm 92:12–15

The righteous will flourish like a palm tree… planted in the house of the Lord.

Psalm 92:12–13 (NIV)

One day our women's group planted seeds in several flower boxes. I was in charge of one flower box. We agreed that once the plants were about 2 inches tall, we would replant them in a garden. But while I was carrying the flower box home, the potting soil shifted, displacing some of the seeds from their original rows. I was certain this project would fail. However, after several days of extra special care my little plants were growing. They even seemed to be growing better than some of the other boxes.

Life can sometimes jostle us about, causing disorientation and placing us in situations that make us vulnerable. But we can take heart in the words of scripture: 'Just as you received Christ Jesus as Lord, continue to live your lives in him, rooted and built up in him, strengthened in the faith as you were taught, and overflowing with thankfulness' (Colossians 2:6–7). With God by our side, we can flourish and face life's challenges.

Prayer: *Almighty God, thank you for the special care you give us. Keep us rooted in the soil of your love so we can grow and prosper. Amen*

Thought for the day: Whether at my best or most vulnerable, God is always with me.

Georgina Domene (La Rioja, Argentina)

Faithful in all things

Read Luke 16:10–13

Better the poor whose way of life is blameless than the rich whose ways are perverse.
Proverbs 28:6 (NIV)

I am currently homeless, and my situation has taught me how much faithfulness and character matter. For instance, I once purchased a coffee and drove away before noticing on my phone that the debit card transaction never went through. When I went back to the coffee shop to explain the situation, I no longer had money on my card. But I promised to pay them after earning some money by trading in recycling. The owner insisted there was no need, but I was determined to pay what I owed, even if this meant skipping a meal.

When we are faithful with the little we have, we demonstrate to God that we can be trusted because we put our faith into action. We show the world that it is better to have an honest character than to be dishonest, whether we live in poverty or possess riches. Not only do we glorify God with our faithfulness, but we share God's love with those we encounter.

God has shown me the importance of being faithful despite poverty and desperation. With Jesus, we can be honest in all things.

Prayer: *Abba, we thank you for your loving discipline. Teach us to be honest in all things so that we can live in accordance with your word. Amen*

Thought for the day: Even my smallest decisions reflect my faith to others.

Jordan Zúñiga (California, USA)

God's voice

Read James 1:22–25

[The Good Shepherd's] sheep follow him because they know his voice.
John 10:4 (NIV)

Following a serious illness, I awoke from a three-week 'sleep' unable to move, talk, swallow or hear. I recovered most of my abilities with time, but my hearing was permanently impaired. I was declared profoundly deaf.

Months later, I tried very powerful hearing aids, and I was shocked when the silence around me was broken. However, most of what I heard was just mechanical noise that made little sense to me and was overwhelming. Amazingly, my husband's voice could cut through that noise, especially when I could focus on his face as he talked. His familiar voice brought me comfort, grounded me and helped me understand what others were saying to me.

Similarly, I believe that God's voice can cut through the frightening noise of the world around us. The more we focus on God and the more familiar we become with God's word, the more readily we can hear God speaking to us each day.

Prayer: *Dear God, may your words of peace and love guide us to do your will today. Amen*

Thought for the day: Focusing on God's voice brings order to my life.

Barbara St. Claire Barton (Tennessee, USA)

A new address

Read Ephesians 2:4–10
By grace you have been saved through faith, and this is not your own doing; it is the gift of God.
Ephesians 2:8 (NRSV)

While on a trip to Lisbon years ago, my wife and I learned a friend at home had passed away. To remember her, we found a nearby church where we could sit and say a prayer. Located at the top of a steep hill, the sanctuary's name was Igreja da Graça – Church of Grace.

As we left the building we noticed an airplane overhead, so my wife checked an app on her phone to see where the plane was coming from and where it was going. A blue circle on the display also told us where we were as it tracked the plane. According to the phone, our location was 'Grace'. I experienced this as a personal message from the Lord: Our new address is grace.

I must admit that I often take the grace of God for granted. But the reality is that the grace of God is given to us freely by the death and resurrection of Jesus. As Paul writes in Ephesians 2:12, before Jesus we had 'no hope' and were 'without God in the world'. Now we have new life in Jesus Christ.

Prayer: *Dear Lord, thank you for Christ's sacrifice and the gift of grace. Help us to embrace this blessing and offer it to others. Amen*

Thought for the day: As a child of God, I have a home in God's grace.

Øyvind Aske (Østfold, Norway)

Behind the scenes

Read Colossians 4:7–16

Epaphras, who is one of you, a servant of Christ Jesus, greets you. He is always wrestling in his prayers on your behalf, so that you may stand mature and fully assured in everything that God wills.
Colossians 4:12 (NRSV)

I once worked for a medical facility where each month the department that showed exemplary efforts was named 'department of the month'. Direct care departments, such as therapy, physicians or nursing, would usually be honoured while administrative areas were overlooked. Then one month, the accounting department where I worked was recognised. Our supervisor had written to the facility's administrator outlining how the behind-the-scenes staff was equally important as those on the front lines. He explained that without our efforts to keep intricate records, ensure timely payroll and navigate insurance billing and collections, the facility would be unable to remain open.

Today's reading from Colossians honours behind-the-scenes workers: Tychicus, Onesimus and Epaphras. The scripture tells us that these are beloved fellow servants in Christ who bring comfort during difficult times. I wonder if the good news about Christ could have been as far-reaching without the support of people like these.

In God's eyes no one is more important than another. We are all equal servants in God's kingdom with our own essential roles.

Prayer: *Dear heavenly Father, please show us where we are needed to serve, and give us the resolve to do our best. Amen*

Thought for the day: What essential role do I fill in serving God?

Monica A. Andermann (New York, USA)

God at work

Read Acts 27:13–26

When neither sun nor stars appeared for many days and the storm continued raging, we finally gave up all hope of being saved.
Acts 27:20 (NIV)

During my son's struggle with addiction I often felt my hope fading. I was afraid he would be lost to this terrible evil. My fear and worry were never-ending and consumed every waking hour. Sometimes I felt I was in the raging storm Paul described in this story from Acts. I was struggling to pray and to trust God.

It must have been like that for the crew and other passengers on the boat with Paul – fearful they would not survive. Without the sun and the moon, they were unable to know where they were. But an angel of God came to Paul and told him not to fear, that all the passengers would survive. With this revelation from God, Paul was able to encourage the passengers and to give them hope.

During my son's struggles, God reassured me that he was at work in my son's life. My worry and fear did not instantly disappear, but God's reassurance gave me the hope I needed to carry on in prayer, asking God's guidance for how best to help my son. I did not always like the answers I received, but with God's help I was assured that my son was in God's hands.

Prayer: *Dear God, when the trials of life are overwhelming, help us to remember our hope is in you and that you will never forsake us. Amen*

Thought for the day: Trusting God creates hope in the heart.

Debbie O'Brien (North Carolina, USA)

God, our shelter

Read Mark 4:35–41

[The Lord] spread out a cloud as a covering, and a fire to give light at night.
Psalm 105:39 (NIV)

In the summer of 2016, a storm came through our area and left a trail of devastation. Our family house was not spared – the roof was extensively damaged and required significant repair. It was a difficult time for many in our community. The force of the storm's impact left us all in a sombre mood for quite a while.

For many of us the walls and roof of our homes give us a sense of security and peace from the weather conditions. While God has not promised us an easy life, God has promised to be our shelter in challenging times.

When the disciples were caught in a storm on the sea, they were indeed fearful; but they found peace because Jesus was there with them. God will surely be here to shelter us as well, leading us through the storms of our lives. We who trust in God are never alone. God has us covered!

Prayer: *Dear God, thank you for covering our lives with your peace and for providing light for us in our darkness. As Jesus taught us, we pray, 'Our Father which art in heaven, hallowed be thy name. Thy kingdom come. Thy will be done, as in heaven, so in earth. Give us day by day our daily bread. And forgive us our sins; for we also forgive every one that is indebted to us. And lead us not into temptation; but deliver us from evil.'* Amen*

Thought for the day: In the visible storm, I will trust the invisible God.

Jim Machuku (Manzini, Eswatini)

*Luke 11:2–4 (KJV)

Running the race

Read Hebrews 12:1–3

Let us run with perseverance the race that is set before us.
Hebrews 12:1 (NRSV)

Running is one of my favourite activities. I feel free and unstoppable when I'm running, and I love the rush of adrenaline. After a run I feel like I just accomplished something huge. Even so, there are some days I don't feel up to it. Finding the motivation to run can be hard, even though I'm always glad when I do it.

Our faith life can be like that too. We are called to pray daily and to follow God's will for us, but saying yes to these things isn't always easy. Sometimes it's hard to wake up early to spend time with God or to release our control and follow God's plan for us.

However, as Christians we are called to pray daily and to follow God's plan for our lives. Hebrews 12:1 encourages us to run God's race with perseverance. The race set before us spans our entire lives and requires us to say yes over and over – praying, showing compassion, going to church and following God's plan for us.

I challenge you to say yes to God – whatever that looks like for you. We can give thanks to God for every opportunity to run the race before us.

Prayer: *Dear Lord, forgive us for the times we don't say yes to you. Give us the courage and strength to say yes more often. Amen*

Thought for the day: Every day brings new opportunities to run the race for God.

Anna Zietz (North Dakota, USA)

On the mend

Read Philippians 4:10–14
What I mean is that we can mutually encourage each other while I am with you. We can be encouraged by the faithfulness we find in each other, both your faithfulness and mine.
Romans 1:12 (CEB)

I was a happy and friendly child, but my attention deficit disorder caused challenges with my schoolwork and in relationships with my schoolmates and teachers. For many years I was bullied, and I was weighed down with a great sense of frustration and rejection. But expressions of concern from a handful of teachers and friends meant so much to me, and my mother, a person of strong faith, always supported me.

When I started high school, the interactions with my schoolmates seemed to get worse – to the point that I wanted to retaliate for the bad experiences I suffered. But even more, I wanted to heal the broken pieces of my life. I knew a little about God from my early years, but at this stage in my life I began to seek God in earnest. I joined the church youth group. My process of healing began when I met those wonderful people who truly reflected the love of Christ and guided and inspired me to learn more about him and his teachings.

Today, I am a university student and a proud Christian. My wounded heart is on the mend, and I am learning the importance of forgiveness as I continue my faith journey to discern God's will for my life.

Prayer: *Merciful God, thank you for loving us and for Jesus' example of forgiveness. Give us courage to stand up for those who suffer abuse and discrimination, knowing that we can do this through Christ who gives us strength. Amen*

Thought for the day: God's unconditional love can heal my wounded heart and spirit.

Ana María Sierra Olivares (Bogotá, Colombia)

Making time

Read Psalm 46

'Be still, and know that I am God! I am exalted among the nations,
I am exalted in the earth.'
Psalm 46:10 (NRSV)

From the moment my alarm goes off until I fall into bed at night, I feel like I am constantly on the go. Between school, work and home, I rush from one place to the next. If I ever have a moment of silence, it's usually filled with a phone call or listening to music. It is no wonder that at the end of the day I feel completely drained!

Psalm 46:10 reminds me that my life is missing intentional silence. It encourages me not just to be still but, in my stillness, to remember that God is in charge. Even Jesus took time away from his ministry to be alone and talk with God.

Throughout the years, I have spent some time in the Middle East, and I've always marvelled at the faithfulness of my Muslim friends. No matter what they are doing, they stop five times a day to spend time with God when they hear the call to prayer. I admire the way they have chosen to be intentional about their prayer lives. Perhaps we can follow the example of our Muslim siblings and set specific times throughout the day to spend time with God – praying, reading scripture and following the example Jesus set for us.

Prayer: *Dear God, you are bigger than our busyness. Help us to set aside the noise of life and to sit in silence with you, even just for a moment. Amen*

Thought for the day: Today I will make time to be still with God.

Michael A. Poe (Florida, USA)

Hidden beauty

Read Philippians 1:1–6

He who began a good work in you will carry it on to completion until the day of Christ Jesus.
Philippians 1:6 (NIV)

I decided to refinish an old piece of furniture that I thought only needed a little work. But stripping off one layer of old stain just led to another layer of stain that I had to strip away in order to uncover the beautiful wood hiding underneath. As I scraped and sanded each small section, I asked myself, *Is this piece of furniture really worth all this hard work or should I just toss it out and get something new?*

I thought about how God works in a similar fashion. God views us as beautiful children, no matter how scarred and damaged we are. God often has to strip away one small part of our lives at a time to reveal the beauty hidden inside. But as with that old piece of furniture, our lives can shine again and be brighter and more beautiful than any new piece of furniture. God can reveal our character and uniqueness.

God will never choose to toss us aside. We just have to allow God to finish the good work in us that has already begun.

Prayer: *Dear God, refinish the parts of our lives that are keeping our true beauty from shining through. Use us always in your service. Amen*

Thought for the day: No matter my scars, God sees the beauty in me.

Debbie Purcell (Florida, USA)

Fruitful grace

Read Jeremiah 17:7–8

Desire first and foremost God's kingdom and God's righteousness, and all these things will be given to you as well.
Matthew 6:33 (CEB)

One morning I arrived at church before anyone else and had to wait. I decided to harvest jujubes from a tree in front of the church and began reflecting on God's grace. I started to view the tree, with its red, green and pale orange fruits, as a symbol of God's grace.

No one planted this tree; it just sprouted here. But it shades the church foyer and provides fruit for the children who come to church. For some time now, only a few people have come to church because of the Covid-19 pandemic. Yet even with no one to water it, this tree has continued to grow and bear fruit while also offering a home to many birds and insects. God has sustained the tree, and the tree sustains the lives of others. What an image of grace!

The tree is blessed as it blesses others. When I am blessed to be able to pick fruits from the tree, I share them with my two children waiting at home. My firstborn has asked me to bring home the fruits every Sunday because it makes him feel as if he and his brother also went to church. Although my children miss going to church, through the jujubes I am able to extend a bit of God's grace to them.

Prayer: *God our provider, teach us to know your grace, even through the smallest fruits that you provide in your creation. Amen*

Thought for the day: What images of God's grace do I see in my community?

Earlie Pasion-Bautista (Isabela, Philippines)

Where I'm meant to be

Read Ephesians 3:7–20

'I know the plans I have for you,' declares the Lord, 'plans to prosper you and not to harm you, plans to give you hope and a future.'
Jeremiah 29:11 (NIV)

When we married, my husband and I had four cats that were allowed to move freely inside and outside of the house. After we moved, we had to keep them in our barn for a month while they acclimated to their new home. Cats have a strong instinct to return to familiar surroundings. Each time I opened the barn door, I had to shut it quickly to block our cats' escape. But one day our cat Muffin got out before I could block her. As I ran after her, she hid under some bushes and meowed in protest. I said, 'Muffin, I know you don't understand, but right now the barn is where you need to be.'

When I later had to change jobs, leaving a position I loved, I complained to God. At my most desperate moment, I recalled the words I had spoken to Muffin and felt God telling me that I was where I needed to be.

So often we can't see God's purpose for us. We complain, bargain and try to escape our situation. But God's goals are not our goals. It may be difficult, but if we believe God is with us, we can trust the one 'who is able to do immeasurably more than all we ask or imagine'.

Prayer: *Dear God, help us to trust that you know where we need to be. Grant us patience with your timing. Amen*

Thought for the day: I can trust that God is with me no matter where I am.

Nancy Dombek (Ohio, USA)

Overcoming despair

Read Psalm 27:1–3

The light shines in the darkness, and the darkness did not overcome it.
John 1:5 (NRSV)

The year 2016 was filled with several life-changing events for my husband and me, the most painful of which was the loss of both our fathers. We were grief-stricken. However, my husband was largely able to carry out his regular responsibilities. He worked as a pastor and served in leadership roles on various levels within our denomination. As he carried on and continued to work, I felt alone, angry and stuck in my grief.

Even though it is my habit to pray every morning, I found it hard to go to God in prayer during this time. One day, I decided I had to do something to break myself out of this pattern. I sat quietly and simply said, 'Thank you, God.' The next day, I thanked God again. With each new day, my time with God grew longer, as did my list of thanks and praise. Each time I expressed gratitude to God, I felt like light was breaking through the darkness that surrounded me. As my spirit of thanksgiving grew, God's light overcame my despair.

These months of grief, anger and prayer taught me that God is always there, even in our darkest times. Honouring our creator with our gratitude reminds us of God's ever-present light and love.

Prayer: *Gracious God, thank you for your abiding presence. Help us to see your light in seasons that feel cloaked in darkness. Amen*

Thought for the day: Today I will tell God what I am grateful for.

Amy Graham (Ohio, USA)

The gift of hope

Read Hebrews 10:23–25
Continue encouraging each other and building each other up, just like you are doing already.
1 Thessalonians 5:11 (CEB)

As a youth pastor, I frequently interact with young Christians struggling with everything from depression to failed relationships. Many come to me seeking help, prayers, advice and comfort.

In listening to their problems, I have come to realise the gift of reassurance. These young students do not want to hear me say why life is unfair to them. They do not want me to explain a solution to their problems. They want a reason to have hope.

And so I remind them that their current problem is a storm that will calm down with time and that God is with them. I tell them that God promises to see them through difficult times and to make their paths straight (see Proverbs 3:5–6). I find that their faith is bolstered and they find the strength to continue through their obstacles when they hear this divine reassurance.

Prayer: *Heavenly Father, thank you for your constant love. Help us to share this love with others by reminding them of the hope that you offer us. Amen*

Thought for the day: When I listen to others' worries, I can offer the gift of hope.

Steve Lawrence (Kiambu County, Kenya)

One body

Read 1 Corinthians 12:12–26

If one member suffers, all suffer together with it; if one member is honoured, all rejoice together with it.
1 Corinthians 12:26 (NRSV)

Several years ago I travelled to Mozambique for a gathering of United Methodist Women. Part of our time was spent with members of the Mozambique Women's Society in the capital city of Maputo, where we studied 1 Corinthians 12. Our cultural backgrounds were very different, and we had a lot to learn from one another. On the third day we studied a variety of prayer practices.

At the end of the session, we had opportunities to express prayer concerns before our corporate prayer, and that is when God revealed the common ground on which we stood. Americans and Mozambicans alike raised concerns about broken families, drug addiction, family and friends affected by HIV and AIDS, domestic abuse, and issues of inequality. As we prayed, we were united with one another and with the Lord.

First Corinthians 12 serves as a reminder that despite different backgrounds and experiences, we are all members of one body in Christ. Our shared needs and dependence on God are revealed when we serve side-by-side in Christ's name.

Prayer: *Dear God, unite us, your children, as one body in Christ so that we may confidently and humbly share the love of Jesus Christ with the world. Amen*

Thought for the day: Though I am only one member, I belong to the body of Christ.

Beth Bronson Troop (Pennsylvania, USA)

What God has done

Read Deuteronomy 26:1–11

'[The Lord] brought us to this place and gave us this land, a land flowing with milk and honey; and now I bring the firstfruits of the soil that you, Lord, have given me.'
Deuteronomy 26:9–10 (NIV)

For more than a year I have been preparing to shift to full-time ministry. I anticipated relying heavily on my savings for the first few years of ministry, but recent changes in the economy have introduced new levels of uncertainty: *Will I be able to afford to quit my current job? Will God provide?* I have considered reducing my tithe to the church in order to pay for my ministry.

In the midst of my worry, my pastor read Deuteronomy 26 before our church's offering, and I was struck by its perspective. Many Bible passages about tithing assure us that God *will* provide. In this passage, the giver declares what God has already done.

As I think about this change in perspective, I realise that God has done great things in my life. God is my creator and redeemer, so I can trust that God's provision will extend into the future. God has called me into full-time ministry. Of this, I am certain. And because God called me, God will provide.

When I centre my thoughts on this truth, the economy no longer worries me. Of course, I have financial needs. But God has been and will be faithful. When I declare how the Almighty has already provided, my heart finds certainty in an uncertain time.

Prayer: *Dear God, help us to remember how you have provided for us in the past and to trust you with the future. Bless our tithes so that they may bless others. Amen*

Thought for the day: I tithe because of what God has already done.

Andrew Michael Ardoin (Louisiana, USA)

Beauty in brokenness

Read Isaiah 43:1–7

Jesus spoke to the people again, saying, 'I am the light of the world. Whoever follows me won't walk in darkness but will have the light of life.'
John 8:12 (CEB)

While walking along a beach where the bush meets the sand, I noticed a beautiful gum tree that had fallen. The tree continued to grow despite being battered by wind and weather. It remained beautiful with its papery soft white bark; and although some branches had died, new growth stretched towards the light.

Like that tree, we are often battered and knocked down by the storms of life. However, like that tree we can remain beautiful and strong in our brokenness. Through the storms that come our way, God can bring new growth into our lives. And as we trust God, our difficulties strengthen us and teach us.

Even when we are broken, we can reach out to Jesus, the light of the world. As we endure our trials, we have the assurance that God has overcome the world (see John 16:33) and that nothing can separate us from God's love. Through our experiences, we become more understanding and compassionate towards others and their struggles. We also learn to draw closer to God and to rely on God in deeper ways than before. In Christ we receive comfort, strength, hope and new spiritual growth.

Prayer: *Loving God, as we reach out to you in our struggles, heal our hearts, bind our wounds and work all things together for our good. Amen*

Thought for the day: When I am surrounded by trouble, I will reach for the light of Christ.

Ann Stewart (South Australia, Australia)

A piece of the puzzle

Read Jeremiah 29:10–14

God revealed his hidden design to us, which is according to his goodwill and the plan that he intended to accomplish through his Son.
Ephesians 1:9 (CEB)

One of my favourite pastimes is quilting, so a friend of mine gave me a jigsaw puzzle with quilts pictured on it. As I sorted and arranged the pieces, I found one piece that was so oddly shaped and of such a peculiar colour that I was sure it was from another puzzle and had mistakenly been put into the box. I set it aside and worked diligently on the puzzle, only to find that there was a piece missing. To my surprise, the piece I had set aside fit perfectly and completed the lovely picture.

As I considered this, it made me think about God's will for us. Just like the oddly shaped puzzle piece, we may feel like we don't fit in with those around us or struggle to understand why God doesn't change our current situation. But just as that piece fit perfectly into the puzzle, we fit perfectly into God's plan. God sees the whole picture while we can see only our piece. Scripture tells us that God has a plan for us. It is up to us to remain faithful, knowing that our lives will fit perfectly into God's picture.

Prayer: *Dear God, help us to remain faithful to you no matter how we see our circumstances. Thank you for your Son, who gives us hope. Amen*

Thought for the day: Today I will trust that God sees the big picture.

Jane Rager (Virginia, USA)

A universal language

Read Acts 2:1–13

After this I heard what seemed to be the loud voice of a great multitude in heaven, saying, 'Hallelujah! Salvation and glory and power to our God.'
Revelation 19:1 (NRSV)

'Hallelujah' is a word used to express praise, joy or thanks – especially to God. It is a word that doesn't need translation. Christians the world over have taken it into their own languages to express joy and praise.

I once attended a wedding in an Orthodox Ethiopian Church. The service was conducted in the Ethiopian language and was a beautiful celebration. However, all I could understand and respond to was 'Hallelujah', since I speak a different African language and English. So when I heard the priest say, 'Hallelujah', and the congregation respond, I also responded with 'Hallelujah!'

It is exciting to realise that all God's children are one big family, praising God in unity of spirit. Even though we may speak different languages, God is happy to receive our praises and joyful shouts of 'Hallelujah!'

Prayer: *We praise you, God, for your faithfulness to us. May we work to count all your children as our family. Hallelujah! Amen*

Thought for the day: 'Hallelujah' is a word that unites us in praise to God.

Funmi Afolabi (Maryland, USA)

Sufficient grace

Read 2 Corinthians 12:1–10
I can do all things through him who strengthens me.
Philippians 4:13 (NRSV)

Since 2004 I have suffered from chronic pain due to an injury to my left leg. I have visited many doctors and tried various treatments and medications, but nothing has helped. I have difficulty walking due to my injury, and I often feel depressed and dejected. I wonder, *Why am I suffering?*

My wife, Sushma, has prayed earnestly for my healing for several years. My family members and many other people are also praying for me. And I have prayed too, but with no change to my physical condition. However, as Paul writes, '[The Lord's] grace is sufficient.'

I face many hardships due to my leg, but I can still get to work and do most of my routine tasks. Sometimes I am even able to forget my injury. I know these graces come from God's goodness, and his mercies are new every morning (see Lamentations 3:23).

Maladies can make us weak physically, but faith can make us strong. When we depend on the Lord, we find new strength. Thank God for the grace and strength we find in Christ.

Prayer: *Merciful God, thank you for your strength and mercy, which never fail us. In Jesus' holy name we pray. Amen*

Thought for the day: God's grace is sufficient for me.

K. D. Mecwan (Gujarat, India)

Worth it

Read Joshua 1:1–9

Keep this Book of the Law always on your lips; meditate on it day and night, so that you may be careful to do everything written in it.
Joshua 1:8 (NIV)

Two bushes stood in our yard, brittle, dry and close to dying. The weather had turned hot, and in the busyness of daily chores I had failed to water the bushes. Could they be saved or would they be victims of my neglect?

I turned on the hose and allowed the water to soak the ground around the bushes twice a day for two days. There was no change. I began to think saving the bushes was impossible. But on the third day I noticed the bushes seemed perkier, greener and not so wilted. I kept watering them. Finally on the fourth day of watering, the two bushes stood tall and healthy. The extra care and watering had been worth it.

Just as the bushes in my yard need care and attention, so does my spiritual life. If I do not prioritise my spiritual growth, my spirit will suffer. Just as plants need water to thrive, my spirit needs attention day after day. Through consistent prayer, Bible study and listening to sermons, I am able to nurture a vibrant and strong faith that can flourish even in challenging circumstances.

Prayer: *Dear God, help us pay attention to what is really important – the care and growth of our spirit. Amen*

Thought for the day: Today I will give attention to my spiritual growth by studying God's word.

Jewell Johnson (Arizona, USA)

Keep it simple!

Read Matthew 6:5–13

*'When you pray, do not keep on babbling like pagans, for they think
they will be heard because of their many words. Do not be like them.'*
Matthew 6:7–8 (NIV)

Sitting beside my goddaughter one evening, I asked if there was anything
she would like me to pray about. 'I'd like you to pray my goldfish never
gets sick,' she replied. I closed my eyes, folded my hands and began,
'Father, we thank you for the joy pets bring us, and we…' My arm was
urgently tugged. I looked up to see her concerned face. 'You're not praying what I asked,' she said with disappointment. 'I asked you to pray my
goldfish doesn't get sick!'

It was one of a number of times where I've felt God speak to me
through the words of a child. I'd been asked to pray a simple prayer, but
added extra words to teach my goddaughter how to pray. Instead she
taught me! Children rarely add lengthy preambles when they ask their
parents for something – they just ask!

It's good to be thankful and to praise God in our prayers, but our words
must come from our hearts. We shouldn't extend our prayers to impress
God. He will see straight through that.

God is our loving Father and wants us to talk to him like a child talks to
a loving parent. Let's be real with God, and allow him to be real with us.

Prayer: *Thank you, Father, that you love us to talk to you and share
our needs. Help us to be honest when we pray and to take time to
listen to you. Amen*

Thought for the day: I can keep my prayers honest and simple.

Catherine Hardcastle (England, United Kingdom)

A prophecy of spring

Read Mark 13:28–31

'Heaven and earth will pass away, but my words will not pass away.'
Mark 13:31 (NRSV)

Winter can be a challenge in Norway. We have only a couple hours of sunshine each day, which means it is largely cold and quiet. Even the birds are silent, with one main exception: the coal tit.

I can be at my forest cabin in January and hear the coal tits singing from the large spruce tree outside. For me, the solitary song of this bird is a prophecy of spring, warmth and sunshine. The snow will melt. Green leaves will grow. Life will return.

Life is not always easy. Disappointments, health challenges and the death of loved ones can feel like the dark, cold, quiet days of a Norwegian winter. We find ourselves wondering: *When will the light return? When will I feel peace?*

In the parable of the fig tree, Jesus tells us that the love of God is always near, even when the darkness overwhelms us. I listen to the coal tits singing in January, and I sense God is near.

Prayer: *Dear Lord, thank you for letting us know that you are near, even in the darkness of winter. We pray in the name of Jesus. Amen*

Thought for the day: In every season, God is near.

Øystein Brinch (Oslo, Norway)

Rest

Rest does not come naturally to me, and I never make it a priority. I love to work; I love to-do lists; I love staying busy. Even my hobbies are physically demanding, and rarely does a vacation involve much downtime. I have two speeds: *stop* and *go*. Early in the summer, I packed my food and gear and set out on a five-day camping trip where I would spend most of my time hiking and cycling. I had made a lengthy list of trails I wanted to hike and set an ambitious goal for the number of miles I would cycle. But on the first full day of my holiday, I tripped over a rock while hiking and broke my foot. Although I was still able to walk, it was painful, and I was mostly out of commission for the rest of the trip. I wasn't happy about it.

The pain in my foot was less than the irritation I felt over the fact that I wouldn't be hiking or cycling anytime soon. I lay in my hammock and read – in a huff because of my circumstances. But then it occurred to me that for the first time in I couldn't remember how long, I was actually relaxing while on holiday. I went to a nearby picnic area and spent time reading one of my favourite poets. Later I sat by a mountain stream for a long time and did nothing but watch the water flow over the rocks. It was peaceful and renewing and, admittedly, wholly unfamiliar. My body felt better and so did my mind.

I reread the chapters in Exodus that recount the events of Mount Sinai, in particular the commandments that God gave to Moses (see Exodus 19–21). Among the commandments was 'Remember the sabbath day, and keep it holy. For six days you shall labour and do all your work. But the seventh day is a sabbath to the Lord your God; you shall not do any work' (Exodus 20:8–10, NRSV). I think this is probably the commandment that I break most often. It's at least one of the easiest for me to break and to justify doing so because my to-do list always seems really important and rest mostly unproductive.

I don't think God breaks our bones to get our attention, but I did learn something from my experience: I can make time for stillness and rest, and nothing bad happens. Nothing important falls through the cracks.

It isn't a slippery slope that leads to idleness or a poor work ethic. It isn't a sign that I am becoming negligent or lazy or irresponsible. Rest is a gift from God that honours God and honours our tired bodies and minds. That God gave us a day for rest is clear evidence to me of how much God cares for us and wants us to care for ourselves. That God gave it to us in the form of a command also tells me that God knew how inclined some of us might be to ignore the gift.

I tend not to realise my need for rest until it's too late. But I am striving to be more proactive by taking regular intervals of time for stillness and renewal. This has taken the form of a nap, finding a nice spot outdoors to read and feel the breeze or having a cup of coffee as I let my mind wander from one thought to the next – all small acts that have made a big difference for me. Rest might look different for each of us depending on our needs. Regardless of the form it takes, I hope we all will find time and a place for the rest that God wants us to have. In Genesis, after creating the heavens and the earth, God rested. If God needed rest, so do we.

QUESTIONS FOR REFLECTION

1 Is making time to rest something that comes easily for you? What does rest look like for you? When have you struggled to find time to rest?

2 When have circumstances forced you to rest? What parts of this experience were uncomfortable for you? How did it change the way you think about rest?

3 Name some scripture verses that speak about rest. Which of these do you find most helpful in terms of your own relationship with rest? Which do you find most challenging?

Andrew Garland Breeden, acquisitions editor

A cloud of witnesses

Read Hebrews 12:1–3

Since we are surrounded by such a great cloud of witnesses, let us throw off everything that hinders.
Hebrews 12:1 (NIV)

I have enjoyed watching videos of choirs from around the world as they sing hymns, some particular to their own cultures and others familiar to almost all Christians. In one video, people from around the world sing 'Amazing Grace', each line sung in a different language – English, Norwegian, German, Hebrew, Chinese, Arabic and many others. The voices come together, using different words but the same melody. In another video, 800 musicians from around the world perform this hymn in English. We see images of them in all their diversity – young and old, percussionists and cellists, individuals with various complexions. Their music inspires and encourages me.

It's the communion of saints, I thought the first time I saw it. In Christ we are connected to one another by this communion of saints, this mighty cloud of witnesses.

Whenever I find myself amid a personal crisis, I'm reassured by the support I feel from all these saints. In every moment we are supported by the prayers of millions who have gone before us yet continue to accompany us. Known and unknown, they're here with us, inviting us into their eternal chorus.

Prayer: *Faithful God, help us to remember to offer support to and receive help from one another. Thank you for the gift of global community. Amen*

Thought for the day: I will remember the saints in my life today.

Lynn Domina (Michigan, USA)

Never too old

Read Genesis 12:1–4

Abram was seventy-five years old when he departed from Haran.
Genesis 12:4 (NRSV)

'Don't you think the people on our church prayer list would like to know that we're praying for them?' my grandmother asked one Sunday morning. And for the next six years, she sent cards to everyone on our church's prayer list. She had to step away from this ministry in 2003 because of health issues, but by that time she had sent more than 12,000 prayer cards!

My grandmother was 78 years old when she began her prayer-card ministry. Her taking on this work later in life makes me think about Abraham, who was 75 years old when God called him. God had a grand purpose for Abraham's life. God would bless all the people of the world through him.

Just as God inspired my grandmother to bless thousands of people, God had plans to bless multitudes through Abraham. What would have happened had Abraham rejected God's call, feeling he was too old to bless anyone? How many people would have missed a blessing from the prayer-card ministry – a ministry that still continues today – if my grandmother had said no to God's call? We are never too old to fulfil God's purposes. And when we faithfully serve, God blesses countless others through us.

Prayer: *Father God, thank you for calling us to serve you, no matter our age. Empower us to do your good work throughout our lives. Amen*

Thought for the day: How is God calling me to serve in this season?

Janine Kuty (Virginia, USA)

Forgiveness

Read Matthew 18:21–35

Then Peter came to Jesus and asked, 'Lord, how many times shall I forgive my brother or sister who sins against me? Up to seven times?' Jesus answered, 'I tell you, not seven times, but seventy-seven times.'
Matthew 18:21–22 (NIV)

When I was in college, it was my habit to use the teachers' chalk to write a short message on the blackboard after class. I hoped my messages would bless someone.

One day my friend erased everything I had written on the blackboard, calling it nonsense. I was furious and walked out of the class, wanting God to punish my friend for his actions. I took my devotional with me when I left, and the topic was on forgiveness. When I was done reading, I felt God ask me to apologise to my friend. It was difficult because I believed he was in the wrong, but I went and apologised for walking away angrily. He smiled, hugged me and gave me a new chalk to write with.

Many times we want people to suffer for doing wrong to us. Sometimes it is difficult to forgive. But in those times, we can remember that Jesus' sacrifice brought us God's forgiveness. In receiving this grace-filled gift of God's love, we can find God's grace sufficient for us to be able to forgive others.

Prayer: *Dear Lord, help us to forgive those who hurt us. Remind us of your forgiveness and grace. Amen*

Thought for the day: I can forgive others because God forgave me first.

Ifenwembi Chinedu (Anambra, Nigeria)

My place of safety

Read Psalm 18:1–6
Keep me safe, my God, for in you I take refuge.
Psalm 16:1 (NIV)

My husband and I are preparing for retirement and a major move, all during the Covid-19 pandemic. The world outside of my home feels chaotic. At the same time, the world inside my home feels full of change and transition. This leaves me feeling depressed. I try to distract myself, but my anxiety and fear are constantly with me.

When my daughter's dog, Dash, is scared, she runs and burrows into the centre of her big yellow pillow. Watching Dash run to the safety of her pillow one day, I thought, *Where is my safe place?* I realised that diversions only push aside my fears and anxieties temporarily. I needed something more solid.

One morning, during another wave of anxiety, I came across Psalm 16:1. I felt the Almighty offering me a safe place. So I shared my fears and anxieties, and God filled me with a sense of comfort and relief. Now when I feel anxiety threaten to overwhelm me, I think of Dash running to her pillow for safety, and I'm reminded that God is my safe place.

Prayer: *Loving God, thank you for your wonderful love. Help us turn to you for comfort and peace when we are overwhelmed. Amen*

Thought for the day: When I feel overwhelmed, God is my safe place.

Jackie Johnson (Arizona, USA)

PRAYER FOCUS: THOSE WHO SUFFER FROM ANXIETY

Never give up

Read 1 Kings 19:1–9

Consider it pure joy, my brothers and sisters, whenever you face trials of many kinds, because you know that the testing of your faith produces perseverance.
James 1:2–3 (NIV)

I have a guava tree in my garden that bears tasty fruit every year. In addition to fruit, this tree produces shade and attracts birds. After a strong windstorm last summer, the guava tree fell. I was reluctant to cut it because it was supported by the structure of the garage and continued to bear fruit. After a year, I reconsidered cutting it down, but I noticed several new shoots emerging from the root of the mother tree. It was regenerating!

I was impressed with the perseverance of this tree. I started to question whether I am as determined when I face challenges. I am living in a period of great financial difficulty and am unemployed. I have already thought about leaving everything and have asked God to take me – similar to the prophet Elijah's request when he was threatened by Jezebel.

But my guava tree has taught me never to give up fighting. It has taught me to trust in the rebuilding that will come from God at the right time.

Prayer: *Faithful God, help us never to give up fighting, because we know that in your timing everything will be made right. In the name of Jesus. Amen*

Thought for the day: I can persevere knowing that God is always with me.

Paulo Fernando Gonçalves de Moura (Rio de Janeiro, Brazil)

PRAYER FOCUS: THOSE WHO ARE UNEMPLOYED

A good work

Read Philippians 1:4–11

All of us, with unveiled faces, seeing the glory of the Lord as though reflected in a mirror, are being transformed into the same image from one degree of glory to another; for this comes from the Lord, the Spirit.
2 Corinthians 3:18 (NRSV)

As an artist, I enjoy the process of creating art as much as the satisfaction of seeing a project finished. I find delight in choosing a colour palette and making each painting unique. My paintings constantly change when I work on them. I often feel that they are an ever-evolving portrayal of life.

I like to live with my paintings for a while and continually see ways to improve and enhance them. I might add a bit of sunlight or a splash of colour in the form of a tiny flower. Often, when I apply the last brush stroke and add my initials to the bottom, I am surprised at how the final outcome has evolved from my initial vision.

When we open our lives to God, we invite the Almighty to change and mould us in ways that improve our lives. As our creator, God moves within us so that we become more like Christ. When the Lord's work in us is complete, we will be astonished by how we have been changed.

Prayer: *Creator God, help us to open our hearts to you and create space for your Spirit to move within us, moulding us into your image. Amen*

Thought for the day: Through the Spirit, I am growing to be more like Christ.

Debbie Rice (Kentucky, USA)

A joyful reunion

Read Matthew 25:1–13

The one who bears witness to these things says, 'Yes, I'm coming soon.' Amen. Come, Lord Jesus!
Revelation 22:20 (CEB)

We were excited when our daughter who lives in Canada informed us that she planned to visit us in India. We were particularly eager to see our 20-month-old grandson, Jonathan. We began to make extensive preparations for Jonathan, as India's climate, culture and food are quite different from Canada's.

Our time as a family was unforgettably enjoyable. The joy of our reunion reminded me of another great reunion, the second coming of the Prince of Peace. Jesus tells us, 'I go to prepare a place for you' and 'I will return and take you to be with me so that where I am you will be too' (John 14:3).

But unlike my daughter's visit, we have no idea when Jesus will come again. It will be wise for us to be prepared like the ten virgins who were ready when their bridegroom came at midnight. Until the Prince of Peace returns, let us wait patiently and expectantly.

Prayer: *Dear Lord, help us always to remember that we are strangers on this earth (see Hebrews 11:13). Teach us to remain faithful as we wait for Jesus to return. We pray as Jesus taught us, 'Our Father in heaven, hallowed be your name, your kingdom come, your will be done, on earth as it is in heaven. Give us today our daily bread. And forgive us our debts, as we also have forgiven our debtors. And lead us not into temptation, but deliver us from the evil one.'* Amen*

Thought for the day: Christ's return will be a joyful reunion.

Ravina Prabodh Diarsa (Gujarat, India)

The love of a cat

Read Romans 8:35–39

Neither height nor depth, nor anything else in all creation, will be able to separate us from the love of God that is in Christ Jesus our Lord.
Romans 8:39 (NIV)

I was never a cat person. And then one morning a hungry kitten showed up at my kitchen door, and I gave it a meatball. That day marked the beginning of my love of cats and led me to a deeper understanding of God's great love for us.

I had always had a hard time accepting the concept of God's unconditional love for us. I couldn't understand how God could continue to love us so much despite our attempts to push God away. Yet the Bible tells us that God loves us in spite of what we do. Living with my cat helped me understand this in a new way, because no matter what she did – run away from me, push me away, all the little annoying things that cats do – I didn't care. I loved her so much that nothing she did harmed my relationship with her. I loved her unconditionally.

I finally realised that this is how God loves us. God loves us, and 'neither height nor depth, nor anything else in all creation will be able to separate us from the love of God that is in Christ Jesus our Lord'. No matter what I do, no matter how many times I push away, God is always there to love me. With the help of a little cat, I finally understood the astounding magnitude of God's great love for us.

Prayer: *Dear Lord, help us to recognise the lessons you teach us through your creation so that we may come to know and love you better. Amen*

Thought for the day: Every creature in God's world has something to teach me.

Ken Roberts (New Jersey, USA)

God's word in our hearts

Read Proverbs 4:20–23
I have hidden your word in my heart that I might not sin against you.
Psalm 119:11 (NIV)

My friend once encouraged me to memorise Bible verses – one beginning with each letter of the alphabet. I took up the challenge and carefully chose 26 passages of scripture. These memorised verses have grown to be an essential part of my faith journey.

I've found that God's word is powerful. It is the truth. As Proverbs 4:22 says, it brings life and healing. When I fill my heart and mind with scripture, it brings me peace and encourages me to worship. If I lie awake at night and can't get back to sleep, I recite these memorised verses to focus my thoughts. If I am anxious during a medical procedure, I think through these verses to calm myself. I have discovered that worship and worry cannot inhabit me at the same time.

Following Jesus' example, we can use scripture to speak truth against temptation, include it in our prayers or say it as a blessing over the lives of those we love. This is all so much easier when we have God's word memorised, living in our hearts. It is a spiritual discipline that I have found to be helpful and encouraging.

Prayer: *Loving Father, thank you for the treasures and truth we find in your life-giving word. Grant us the strength and fortitude to meditate on your scripture, study it and memorise it. Amen*

Thought for the day: I can find healing and new life with God's word in my heart.

Ann Stewart (South Australia, Australia)

'Kindness is everything'

Read Matthew 25:31–40

'I was hungry and you gave me food to eat. I was thirsty and you gave me a drink. I was a stranger and you welcomed me. I was naked and you gave me clothes to wear. I was sick and you took care of me. I was in prison and you visited me.'
Matthew 25:35–36 (CEB)

In recent years, I have noticed a rise in social messaging around kindness. For example, 'Be kind' has been added to email signatures, social media statuses, T-shirts and face masks. And 'Kindness is everything' has become a new rallying cry for social justice.

In Matthew 25:35–36, Jesus shows the eternal importance of Christian kindness: feeding the hungry and quenching people's thirst; welcoming the stranger and clothing the naked; caring for the sick and visiting the imprisoned. These kindnesses are more than a 'nice' way of being. They are a communal commitment to meeting every human's basic needs. These acts mean everything to many people who are in desperate need. And radical kindness opens the door to blessings, eternal life and the kingdom of God. When we act in kindness and care for those who are in need, we care for Jesus.

If we are truly followers of Christ, we must understand that kindness is everything – for those in need and for our own souls. Without this understanding, attempts at a ministry of justice are incomplete. As a follower of Jesus, I think 'Kindness is everything' is a mantra all Christians can rally around.

Prayer: *Lord Jesus, show us how to live out your truth that kindness is everything in the midst of these challenging times. Amen*

Thought for the day: I can do justice through acts of Christian kindness.

Siera Grace Toney (District of Columbia, USA)

The story of Moses

Read Exodus 1:22—2:10
After the child had grown up, [Moses' mother] brought him back to Pharaoh's daughter, who adopted him as her son. She named him Moses, 'because,' she said, 'I pulled him out of the water.'
Exodus 2:10 (CEB)

The story of Moses reminds me of God's grace and care. I am particularly moved by the way God saved Moses from death according to Pharaoh's decree, keeping him in the Nile River until he was spotted and rescued by Pharaoh's daughter. What an unlikely outcome that Pharaoh's daughter would put aside her father's decree, ask Moses' mother to nurse him and then raise Moses as her son! The appearance of Pharaoh's daughter and her discovery of the baby were not mere coincidences; they were acts of God, part of an amazing plan to save Moses.

Moses' story encourages us to think of all the acts of God in our own lives. It invites us to ponder how we show appreciation for God's saving grace upon our lives and the lives of our loved ones. How do we explain God's love for us and God's work of salvation through Jesus Christ? The amazing acts of God are limitless.

We could never number the blessings God has provided for us. But we can trust that just as God offered grace to Moses, God will surely help and keep us.

Prayer: *Dear God, thank you for your love and saving grace. May we never take your presence with us for granted. Amen*

Thought for the day: Today I will look for God's grace in my circumstances.

B'Kolly (Lagos, Nigeria)

PRAYER FOCUS: GRATITUDE FOR GOD'S PROVISION

Another try

Read Lamentations 3:21–24

The steadfast love of the Lord never ceases, his mercies never come to an end; they are new every morning.
Lamentations 3:22–23 (NRSV)

Last week during a friendly round of golf, I hit an errant drive. I exclaimed, 'Man, I wish I could have that one back! I'm sure I could do better.' Fortunately for me, my golfing partner said, 'Give it another try.' So I did, and I hit the ball long and straight down the fairway.

How many times in our lives have we wished to correct a mistake or retract an unpleasant word or action that hurt someone? Many times I've thought about how a certain situation might have turned out differently if I had put myself in the other person's shoes for a moment before reacting in an unwarranted, negative way.

We are fortunate that our loving God understands the human heart and mind. No matter how many times we miss the mark, God gives us an unlimited supply of chances to use for correcting our errant actions, while forgiving us as we try to learn from our mistakes.

Prayer: *Dear God, bless us with courage and discernment to do what is right according to your will. Amen*

Thought for the day: God's forgiveness is always accompanied by another chance.

Jerry Albritton (Kentucky, USA)

PRAYER FOCUS: THOSE IN NEED OF ANOTHER CHANCE

Unexpected blessings

Read Jeremiah 17:7–8

Give thanks to the Lord, for he is good; his love endures forever.
Psalm 106:1 (NIV)

We have a courtyard garden with more than 80 daffodil bulbs. In the late winter and early spring the courtyard is filled with beautiful yellow blooms. This year we gave the flowers away to friends who needed cheering up, so we thought we would have to wait another year to see the daffodils again. Imagine our surprise when recently we discovered seven more yellow buds poking up among the green leaves, brightening our garden and our lives.

God's blessings are like those late-blooming daffodils – sometimes unexpected but always a special encouragement to us. They remind us that God is always here for us and cares for us constantly, especially in difficult circumstances. Life can change overnight, but blessings such as the smile of a grandchild, a beautiful garden, a sunny day or the kindness of friends can give us hope. We can always find blessings for which to thank God.

Prayer: *O God, thank you for your constant love and blessings. Help us to share them with others. In Jesus' name. Amen*

Thought for the day: God surprises me each day with simple blessings.

Margaret Martin (Australian Capital Territory, Australia)

Come as you are

Read John 3:16–18
God didn't send his Son into the world to judge the world, but that the world might be saved through him.
John 3:17 (CEB)

The billboard near the highway displayed a photograph of a young Muslim woman with a head covering. The caption read, 'We are fully inclusive.' I felt a tinge of offence at the community college's ad. *Why the push to accept Islam?* Then, Jesus spoke to my heart, 'I am fully inclusive.' The juxtaposition of Jesus' words to my reaction left me stunned. I felt his sadness at my failure to represent him; his words had exposed my bigotry.

Jesus is unbiased; he unreservedly welcomes every human being, regardless of religion or background. But like the Pharisees of Jesus' day, I was demanding that people meet certain criteria in order for God to receive them and love them. God deeply loves and values every person, and the Son of God paid the ultimate price for *all* people.

God invites us to come as we are. In the embrace of God's extravagant love and acceptance there is redemption, forgiveness and peace. This is the good news for all!

Prayer: *Loving God, thank you for accepting us as we are. Reveal any prejudice within us so we can repent and align our hearts and attitudes with yours. Amen*

Thought for the day: Jesus sees everyone through eyes of lavish love.

Donna Y. Gurr (Oregon, USA)

In times of uncertainty

Read Romans 5:1–6

Hope does not disappoint us.
Romans 5:5 (NRSV)

The Tokyo Olympics were scheduled to begin in 2020, but due to the rise of Covid-19, Japan's government proclaimed a state of emergency and the games were postponed. We were suddenly thrust into quarantine in our homes. During that time my pregnant wife was hospitalised for over two months prior to giving birth. While she was hospitalised, visitation was prohibited.

Meanwhile, our daughter and I stayed home where she participated in unfamiliar remote schooling. And because her mother, who understood her best, was hospitalised, she struggled even more.

As our family contended with these various issues, I continued to read *The Upper Room*. My study of God's word and reading the testimony of believers who also were leaning on God gave me hope. Then, when our second daughter was born, her new life deepened my hope. With purity of heart, she cried when her stomach was empty. And when satisfied, she smiled and became visibly peaceful. Seeing her natural trust in our provision, I realised that I could also, with assurance, express my needs to God. I thank God for the grace given me in my time of need.

Prayer: *O God, lead our families to become united. Enable us to stay close to you, no matter what we are facing. In Jesus' name. Amen*

Thought for the day: Every day I will give thanks for God's grace.

Kenichi Kurokawa (Tokyo, Japan)

Necessary gifts

Read 1 Corinthians 12:4–11

To each is given the manifestation of the Spirit for the common good.
1 Corinthians 12:7 (NRSV)

I was sitting in the dining room with some other residents at our senior retirement centre. We were talking about previous holidays with family and friends and what our particular job had been in preparing the holiday meal. For some, it was making the pies. For others, it was preparing the stuffing with either corn bread or white bread. My job was making fresh cranberry sauce.

As I reflected on this conversation, I realised that the worship and work of the church is much like preparing a holiday meal. We all have gifts to share. And we all receive gifts from others. During a worship service, the preacher preaches, the choir sings, the reader shares scripture and the acolyte lights the candles. During the week, members pray for those who have submitted requests, Sunday school teachers prepare lessons and pray for their students, the custodians make sure the church is ready for meetings and someone always makes sure the coffee is hot and the donuts are out!

Whether it's our family or faith community, each person offers a gift that is necessary to the whole body. With joy, we get to share our gifts and receive the gifts of others.

Prayer: *Dear Lord, give us this day our daily bread and inspire us to share it. Amen*

Thought for the day: God calls me to share my gifts joyfully.

Sharon Christen (Texas, USA)

PRAYER FOCUS: GRATITUDE FOR THE GIFTS OTHERS SHARE WITH ME

The good shepherd

Read Luke 15:1–7

'Suppose someone among you had one hundred sheep and lost one of them. Wouldn't he leave the other ninety-nine in the pasture and search for the lost one until he finds it?'
Luke 15:4 (CEB)

As a child, the parable of the lost sheep was my favourite, and I often asked my parents to tell it to me at bedtime. I found the story thrilling – the shepherd counting the sheep, realising that one was missing and going out to look for it despite the dangers. I always worried about the lost sheep, but I felt such relief and happiness when it was brought back to safety. The message of this parable still brings me strength today.

As I think of the children around the world who face countless dangers and challenges, I remember our good shepherd, who does not give up on us. Even in the face of challenges and problems that cause us fear, we can count on Christ's faithfulness. We are called to share Christ's love with others, and children need someone to walk with them and introduce them to the faithful shepherd. My hope for all children is that when they feel insecure or afraid, they will know that Jesus, their good shepherd, is nearby – coming to bring them hope and peace.

Prayer: *Merciful God, make us sensitive to the needs of children. Help us to share your love with them so they may be certain they are never alone. In the name of Jesus. Amen*

Thought for the day: How will I help children in need in my community today?

Elci Lima (São Paulo, Brazil)

Even when

Read Matthew 17:14–20

[Jesus] replied, 'Truly I tell you, if you have faith as small as a mustard seed, you can say to this mountain, "Move from here to there," and it will move. Nothing will be impossible for you.'
Matthew 17:20 (NIV)

The following was written on a wall during the Holocaust by an unknown author: 'I believe in the sun even when it is not shining, I believe in love even when I cannot feel it, I believe in God even when he is silent.' The writer describes faith so well – believing in the unseen. The first time I read the inscription, I contemplated how someone could have such faith during such a horrific time. Who was this person? What happened to them?

In the scripture reading for today, the disciples wanted to know why they could not heal someone the way Jesus did. Jesus replied that it was because they lacked faith. They did not believe they could heal, so they were unable to. Jesus goes on to say that you only need a little faith, the size of a mustard seed, to do great things like move mountains. Sometimes our faith is tested; sometimes God seems silent; sometimes our prayers seem to go unanswered. But just as the sun still exists when we cannot see it, God is still with us even when God seems silent.

Prayer: *Dear God, help us to know you are with us even when you seem silent. Strengthen our faith when we feel abandoned. Amen*

Thought for the day: I have faith today that God is present in my life.

Steve Wakefield (Alabama, USA)

Paid

Read Ephesians 2:1–10
*You are saved by God's grace because of your faith. This salvation is
God's gift. It's not something you possessed.*
Ephesians 2:8 (CEB)

One of the benefits of my employment as a professor at a public university is the free tuition for children of employees. My daughter decided
to enrol at this university and take advantage of the scholarship. We
reviewed the administrative processes and documentation needed to
register online for the coming year. As we entered our personal data,
there was also a required field in the system to post the registration fee.
At this point, a message appeared in the centre of our screen: 'Paid'. We
owed nothing; my daughter could look forward to the semester without
incurring debt.

Drawing a parallel, when we accept Jesus as our Lord and Saviour, the
slate is wiped clean. The sacrifice Christ made for us on the cross makes
it possible for us to have eternal life. By faith, we are beneficiaries of the
fullness of God's mercy. We can rest secure in the knowledge that the
message on our slate will read: 'Paid'.

Prayer: *Faithful God, great is your mercy and greater still your love for
us – a love so great that your Son, Jesus, died on the cross to pay for
our sins and grant us eternal life. Thank you, Lord! Amen*

Thought for the day: I am the beneficiary of God's love and mercy.

Palmira Valenzuela (Nuevo León, Mexico)

Honest emotions

Read Psalm 42

Why, my soul, are you downcast? Why so disturbed within me? Put your hope in God, for I will yet praise him, my Saviour and my God.
Psalm 42:5 (NIV)

There are times when I wake up discouraged. There is no particular reason for me to feel this way, but nonetheless the feeling is overwhelmingly there. I struggle to find motivation and purpose. As a result, I become angry with myself. I think, *I should be thankful! God has blessed me with so much.* I berate myself and try to fix the way I feel. When that doesn't work, I feel ashamed that I have a comfortable life but still feel sad.

Psalm 42 reminds me that many people in the Bible also felt discouraged. As verse 5 demonstrates, sometimes they felt disheartened for no apparent reason, too. This psalm teaches me that it is human to feel discouraged sometimes. But no matter the cause, we can be honest with God about our emotions. God does not expect us always to be happy. Our creator just wants us to be honest. The Almighty hears our cries and is ready to comfort us when we faithfully open our hearts.

Prayer: *Dear Lord, we cry out to you in our discouragement. You are our help, our peace and our comfort. You are the source of our hope. Amen*

Thought for the day: When I feel discouraged, I will go to God.

Jennifer Brigandi (Ontario, Canada)

Under his wings

Read Psalm 91:1–4

He will cover you with his feathers, and under his wings you will find
refuge; his faithfulness will be your shield and rampart.
Psalm 91:4 (NIV)

Our family kept a few chickens when I was a child. We grew fond of them, giving each one a name, and they became very tame. Best of all, those hens produced fluffy yellow chicks, which gave us even more fun. Sometimes a car drove up close to where the chickens pecked and scratched. Immediately the mother hen would call her brood, and they'd dash to safety under her wings.

It's a picture which stays with me, and it is beautifully expressed in Psalm 91:4. What safer place could there be than the shelter of God's wings, both for now and for all the times to come? With concern, Jesus urges us not to miss out on such vital security: 'How often I wanted to gather your people together, just as a hen gathers her chicks under her wings. But you didn't want that' (Matthew 23:37, CEB). Solemn words to remember.

Prayer: *Lord, help us to find our greatest security in you. Amen*

Thought for the day: There is no better shelter than Jesus.

Elaine Brown (Scotland, United Kingdom)

Peppermint

Read Mark 4:30–34
The kingdom of God is within you.
Luke 17:21 (KJV)

As I read again the parable of the mustard seed this morning, I am reminded of the time I spent in my garden last week planting seeds. The peppermint seeds were the smallest of the bunch. But because peppermint grows and spreads quickly, I know these little seeds will eventually take over my garden.

The kingdom of God works in a similar way. When we receive Jesus into our hearts, we wake up to a whole new way of loving God, ourselves and others. The seed of this transformation is small at the beginning, but as we follow Jesus day by day, it grows roots, gains strength and spreads everywhere. And just like a garden, the seed of the kingdom of God also needs to be nurtured. We can do this by reading the Bible, praying and practising faithful obedience to God.

Now every time I look at my peppermint plant and water it, I will remember that my soul also needs spiritual watering so that the kingdom of God will grow roots and spread – in me and through me to the world.

Prayer: *Creator God, thank you for the transformation that is possible through Jesus Christ. Guide us so that we can nurture the seed of your kingdom that lives in our hearts. Amen*

Thought for the day: The kingdom of God lives in me.

Andreea Nicolae (England, United Kingdom)

The forgotten bike

Read Psalm 142

'Be strong and courageous. Do not be afraid or terrified because of them, for the Lord your God goes with you; he will never leave you nor forsake you.'
Deuteronomy 31:6 (NIV)

As I hurried by, I saw that the bike was still there – small, pink and white, probably once a girl's greatest treasure. Now it sat unsecured and forgotten, strangely out of place in the heart of a busy college campus.

The forgotten bike reminds me that there's lots of work to be done to help those who are forgotten in this world: the people without homes, tucked away in hidden corners of our communities; those who are housebound and longing for company; and those who are sick, incarcerated, widowed or orphaned all come to mind.

Many times Jesus recognised people that others had largely dismissed: the woman caught in adultery (see John 8:1–11); the man with an unclean spirit living among the tombs (see Mark 5:1–20), tax collectors (see Luke 19:1–10) and the man with leprosy (see Mark 1:40–45).

God calls each of us to do what we can to help those in our communities who need a kind word, a thoughtful note, a meal or a prayer. We all can do something that says we haven't forgotten. It can make all the difference in the world.

Prayer: *God of all, help us to ease the suffering of those who feel forgotten. In Jesus' name. Amen*

Thought for the day: Small efforts offered with compassion can make a big difference.

D. Gerow Baker (Oklahoma, USA)

Forecourt frenzy

Read Luke 6:32–36

'Love your neighbour as yourself.'
Leviticus 19:18 (NIV)

I could sense my neighbour's concern as she spoke about the fuel crisis. The prospect of putting petrol into her car was looking pretty remote. Pru worked for the NHS, and without petrol she couldn't visit her patients. It felt like the last straw when the woman ahead of her topped up the tank of her gleaming roadster and disappeared into the diner. Cars built up on the forecourt, as the empty vehicle blocked access to the petrol pumps.

As tempers frayed and drivers began to toot, Pru walked towards the pay desk, hoping to resolve the issue. But as she passed the diner, she was stunned to see the driver of the empty car sitting at a table tucking into a pizza.

'And how did you react?' I asked.

'It seemed like an act of God,' said Pru. 'When the man at the pay desk noticed the problem, he put out a call on the PA system.'

My friend had been spared from having a potentially difficult confrontation. I couldn't help thinking about the goodness of God and the way he provides for all our needs.

Prayer: *Lord, as we struggle to control our feelings of frustration, help us to realise that a little self-control can defuse the most frustrating circumstances.*

Thought for the day: 'Love covers over a multitude of sins' (1 Peter 4:8).

Pauline Pullan (England, United Kingdom)

Healing through Christ

Read Philippians 4:10–13

I can endure all these things through the power of the one who gives me strength.
Philippians 4:13 (CEB)

As I write this, I am 11 months into my journey to sobriety. It has been a difficult pathway with many challenges, but I am encouraged by Philippians 4:13. These words aid me in my recovery from addiction and empower me in my daily activities. Believing in the power of Christ makes all the difference. Although my circumstances overwhelm me at times, I gain strength from Christ.

There was a time when I thought that things would never improve, and I would have to abuse substances for the rest of my life just to cope. But Christ has given me the confidence to stay committed in my recovery and seek the spiritual, physical and psychological healing I need. I know that I would have remained in the bondage of addiction if I did not have Christ as my source of strength. When we fix our minds on Christ and believe that through him all things are possible, it may not be easy, but Christ will strengthen us to push through.

Prayer: *Dear God, help us to see you at work in all things. Increase our faith in your providence. Amen*

Thought for the day: In good times and bad, I will praise the Lord.

Remigio Angelo Dingashe (Northern Cape, South Africa)

Under construction

Read 2 Corinthians 4:16–18

For our light and momentary troubles are achieving for us an eternal glory that far outweighs them all.
2 Corinthians 4:17 (NIV)

Living for a while in a strange city, I used to visit a museum that was undergoing renovations. Those galleries that were open were reached through a long temporary windowless tunnel, which led from the door to the back stairs.

One day I went in and the tunnel was gone, and the restoration of the area where it had once been was finished. My breath was taken away by the beauty, the light and the sheer size of the space I was standing in. Something totally unimagined.

Months later I became ill, and in prayer the Lord brought the memory of this to my mind. At first I hoped it was a promise of physical healing, and that helped for a while. But as the years have passed without change, I have begun to see it as a visual reassurance of the truth of these verses. That however heavy our load, however drab the tunnel we may be walking through, when nothing seems to be changing, God is working, unseen and in ways we cannot even imagine, to restore us and all his beloved creation.

And one day all will be revealed, and we will stand amazed at the bright and wondrous things he has done. And we will find that nothing has been wasted.

Prayer: *Lord, please help us when we carry heavy loads, and encourage us with the thought that one day we will see the glory that far outweighs them all. Amen*

Thought for the day: How can I let the unseen and eternal things find space in my heart and mind today?

Helen Vincent (England, United Kingdom)

First Sunday of Advent

Read Psalm 143:7–10

'The Lord your God is with you, the Mighty Warrior who saves. He will take great delight in you; in his love he will no longer rebuke you, but will rejoice over you with singing.'
Zephaniah 3:17 (NIV)

Christmas is usually my favourite season, and I look forward to it with great anticipation. Many years ago, though, I was filled with emptiness despite the approaching holiday. A relationship with a man I loved and had planned my future with had fallen apart that autumn. All of a sudden, my life felt aimless.

I spent the holidays at home with my widowed father that year. One drab day in late December, I looked through his kitchen window and felt that the overcast weather mirrored my emotions. When I turned around, I noticed my father's appointment calendar. On the date I had arrived, he had written my flight information. Underneath it was a note: 'Lisa home. Happy, happy!'

Suddenly, I was overwhelmed by the impact of his love. How could I feel so empty knowing that my presence caused my father so much joy? On a deeper level, I was reminded that I also have a heavenly parent who loves me and rejoices over me, even more than my earthly parent does. I knew this love would carry me through my break-up and any other hard times that I might face. Now, decades later, I can say that God's love continues to sustain me.

Prayer: *Gracious Lord, thank you for your unfailing love, which is the anchor for our lives. Amen*

Thought for the day: Like a loving parent, God rejoices over me.

Lisa Stackpole (Wisconsin, USA)

Removing the dust

Read John 15:1–8

Abide in me, and I in you. As the branch cannot bear fruit of itself, except it abide in the vine; no more can ye, except ye abide in me.
John 15:4 (KJV)

For many days, my computer kept losing power. No matter how many times I plugged it into the electrical outlet, the computer would start up then abruptly stop. Someone came and checked the battery, but it was fine. I removed the plug again and noticed it was coated in particles of dust. When I removed the dust and plugged it in again, the computer quickly lit up and ran normally.

This experience reminded me of our connection to Christ, the true vine. Sometimes we allow unneeded, even dangerous elements, such as fear, worry, unkind thoughts, envy, hatred or greed, to build up in our minds and hearts. These get in the way of our connection to Christ. When we surrender all these matters to God through prayer and repentance, God will remove them and free us to live in his power.

Prayer: *God our Father, help us to keep our minds fixed on you so that everything that blocks our connection to you may be removed. In Jesus' name. Amen*

Thought for the day: When I clear my mind of negative thoughts, God's power flows more freely in me.

Annette Poitier (The Bahamas)

Inspiring kindness

Read Matthew 13:3–23

'The seed falling on good soil refers to someone who hears the word and understands it. This is the one who produces a crop, yielding a hundred, sixty or thirty times what was sown.'
Matthew 13:23 (NIV)

When I think about bearing fruit for Christ, I am reminded of a story I once heard on the news. At the drive-through window of a coffee shop, a customer spontaneously paid for the order of the next car in line. It was an act of pure kindness and generosity. When the next car reached the window and discovered that the person in front had already paid, they were so touched that they, in turn, paid for the order of the next person in line.

This chain of generosity continued for more than 200 people. Upon discovering that the person ahead had paid for their order, each customer was inspired to pay for the next person's. The kindness was contagious. I imagine that the person who initiated this beautiful chain of love had no idea of the fruit that this one act of kindness would bear. This incident inspires me to obey God in faith and not worry so much about the outcome. I am convinced that when we obey Christ's command to love others, it will bear fruit, even if we don't personally see the results.

Prayer: *Dear God, help us to show spontaneous acts of love every day. Amen*

Thought for the day: With God's help, my single act of kindness can inspire many more.

George T. Wilkerson (North Carolina, USA)

Reason to celebrate

Read John 6:47–59

'I am the living bread that came down from heaven. Whoever eats of this bread will live forever; and the bread that I will give for the life of the world is my flesh.'
John 6:51 (NRSV)

When I was a child, though my family was Christian, we didn't celebrate Christmas. I remember seeing families going to church on Christmas Eve and Christmas morning, singing carols, gathering to celebrate and doing all the merry things; but not us.

When I asked why we celebrated the death and resurrection of Jesus but not his birth, I was told that Jesus wasn't born on 25 December; but we didn't celebrate his birth on any other day either. It's like he was never born.

Now as an adult, I am learning to fully celebrate Christmas, embracing it as a time to remember Jesus' birth and his willingness to dwell among us. Celebrating Christmas reminds me of the forgiveness and redemption we have received through Jesus' sacrifice. This festive season gives me the perfect opportunity to share with others all I have received from the Bread of Life – material and spiritual – and to invite them to feast on the living bread of Jesus with me.

Prayer: *Dear Jesus, thank you for coming into the world. We love you and pledge to follow you always. Amen*

Thought for the day: Christmas celebrates God's gift of Jesus to us all.

Adhiambo E. Ochien'g (Nairobi, Kenya)

'Delete!'

Read Matthew 6:12–15

Jesus said, 'Father, forgive them, for they do not know what they are doing.'
Luke 23:34 (NIV)

Sitting in a roadside cafe in Nice on the morning of our ruby wedding anniversary, my husband, Jim, was taking a photo of the beautiful beach. A group of five soldiers were crossing the road, and as they got near to us the lead soldier pointed at Jim and his camera and shouted 'Delete!' (The country was in a state of high security alert at the time.) Startled by the unexpected command, Jim accidentally deleted all of our holiday photos, including a special one of both of us that the gîte owners had taken.

I was furious with the soldier, but immediately I was reminded of Jesus' words from the cross, 'Father, forgive them, for they do not know what they are doing.' Jesus did not withhold his forgiveness when he suffered immeasurably greater pain at the hands of soldiers than what I had just experienced. When I followed Jesus' example and forgave the man, a tremendous peace flooded my soul.

In the end, God restored to us what was lost – we revisited the places where we had taken photos and the gîte owners took an even better photo of us, this time with a bunch of white roses they gifted to us.

Prayer: *Lord Jesus, by your Holy Spirit please help us to forgive others and release them into your abundant grace. Amen*

Thought for the day: God has 'deleted' all of my sins.

Jenny Farquhar (England, United Kingdom)

On God's mind

Read Psalm 8

What are human beings, that you exalt them, that you take note of them, visit them each morning, test them every moment?
Job 7:17–18 (CEB)

I remember in high school when we were learning basic science. We were given a cup with soil and a bean seed inside to take home. We were assigned the task of caring for and observing its growth. Each day I would go to the window to water my plant and make sure it was getting enough sunlight. I was happy to see how the plant responded to the care I gave it.

My plant-tending experience helps me relate to this verse: 'What are human beings, that you exalt them, that you take note of them, visit them each morning, test them every moment?' God is thinking of me. I am on God's mind every day.

Just as I carefully tended my plant, God cares for us so that we lack nothing in our growth towards fullness of life. Sometimes our growth can be a painful process. But God knows that pruning is a vital part of creating a healthy, mature life – be it a plant or a human being. In the end, God is always working to make something good out of our lives.

Prayer: *Thank you, God, for your constant care and attention to our lives. Nurture our growth with your love so that we may live joyfully. Amen*

Thought for the day: I am on God's mind every day.

Olanike Adenuga (Lagos, Nigeria)

By God's grace

Read 1 John 4:7–12

'Therefore I tell you, do not worry about your life, what you will eat or drink; or about your body, what you will wear. Is not life more than food, and the body more than clothes?'
Matthew 6:25 (NIV)

Several years ago, I had an eating disorder that threatened to destroy everything I held dear. During my darkest days, I became a shadow of my former self. I lied to my parents, isolated myself from my friends and communicated only in cascading tears or hostile outbursts. I abandoned the Lord. However, the Lord never abandoned me.

I eventually entered a residential treatment centre. One night, God led me to today's quoted scripture verse, telling me not to worry about food, as the eating disorder made me so inclined to do, or about my body, against which I harboured such hatred. The words God spoke to me that night meant something very different to me than what they meant to the crowds Jesus first delivered them to. And yet mercifully, God led me to them at the very moment I needed them most. God gave me courage to pursue recovery and was with me every step of the way.

Today, by the grace of God and the support of my family, I am free from my eating disorder. But when temptation returns, I think of that night when God provided what I needed most: God's unconditional love.

Prayer: *Loving God, thank you for leading us to your word and speaking to us through it. Help us not to worry but to trust in your love. Amen*

Thought for the day: God always provides what I need most: unconditional love.

Eliza Smith (Tennessee, USA)

Second Sunday of Advent

Read Isaiah 9:1–7

Glory to God in the highest, and on earth peace, good will towards men.

Luke 2:14 (KJV)

In Sri Lanka, the island nation where I was born, Christmas is celebrated by all people regardless of their background or religion. When we read the angel's praise in Luke 2:14, we see that the angel does not exclude anyone. Christmas is an invitation to everyone to hear the good news of Jesus' birth.

Long before the first Christmas, Jesus' birth was predicted by the prophet Isaiah. And in Matthew 1:23 we read that in fulfilment of Isaiah's prophecy, Jesus is to be called Emmanuel, which means 'God with us'. In these scary and confusing times, the word 'Emmanuel' resonates powerfully in my soul. God is with us all!

Christmas offers us a time to focus on the nature of God, the goodness of creation, the sacredness of all people, and the ways the holy and the secular mingle. God is with us in joy and sorrow, in poverty and wealth, in waking and in sleeping. God makes us merry, bears our pain, keeps our peace and reconciles us. God is truly with us always.

Prayer: *Eternal God, thank you for giving us Emmanuel, a reminder of your everlasting presence. Help us to see you in every part of creation in this holy season. Amen*

Thought for the day: This Christmas I will seek unity with the people around me.

S. Thevanesan (New York, USA)

Never without help

Read Genesis 28:10–17

Your way of life should be free from the love of money, and you should be content with what you have. After all, [the Lord] has said, I will never leave you or abandon you.
Hebrews 13:5 (CEB)

I remember the day I received the email telling me that I had been accepted to a master's degree programme in a different country. I was sitting in the airport when my new reality sank in. I was leaving my continent, my family and my friends and would be on my own for two years. In my first class, I remember feeling like I had no idea what was going on. I wondered, *Will I even make it? Will I have anyone to help me?*

During that season, I would sit in my room and speak the words from Hebrews 13:5 to myself to help me be conscious of God's presence in my life. The more I did this, the more it helped me through each day – even when I felt stuck, nervous, confused, alone and homesick. By God's grace, I was surrounded by people who helped me with my coursework. I met people who helped me feel at home in a strange country. I was not alone.

God's word can be trusted. No matter our situation or where we are, we can always rely on God to be right here with us, helping us through.

Prayer: *Dear Lord, thank you for always being with us. Help us each day to be attentive to your presence. Amen*

Thought for the day: I am never without help because God is with me.

Selina Machado (Blantyre, Malawi)

Resurrection hope

Read Isaiah 61:1–4

[The Lord] has sent me… to give… oil of joy in place of mourning,
a mantle of praise in place of discouragement.
Isaiah 61:1, 3 (CEB)

On a particularly beautiful Easter Sunday afternoon, I was lying on a grassy hillside not far from where I lived. The sun was warm, and fluffy white clouds floated in a bright blue sky.

It had been an extraordinarily hard 18 months, and I was feeling battered in body, mind and spirit. In particular, it had been many months since I had been able to walk more than a few yards without becoming exhausted. I was weary and discouraged. I longed for resurrection – for the same power that raised Jesus from the dead to fill me so that I could walk, run and explore God's creation more fully. But that felt like a far-off dream.

Then in the warm April sunshine, I sensed God telling me that this dream could become reality. At first I dismissed it as wishful thinking. However, as joy in the day's beauty welled up inside me, so did hope. I couldn't resist getting up on my feet to see how far I could go.

Thus began a healing process that continues to this day. Mourning turned to joy, and discouragement turned to praise. Weakness slowly turned to strength. My hope and faith were renewed as I began to experience God's resurrecting power in a new way.

Prayer: *Resurrecting God, you are the source of all life and goodness. Thank you for bringing us new joy and hope through your resurrecting love. Amen*

Thought for the day: What hope does the resurrection offer me today?

Rosalind Smith (Cluj, Romania)

Divine examples

Read John 6:5–13

I know what it is to be in need, and I know what it is to have plenty.
I have learned the secret of being content in any and every situation,
whether well fed or hungry, whether living in plenty or in want.
Philippians 4:12 (NIV)

My mother grew up in a large family whose meals came mostly from their own land and animals. They were not poor, but they had as many mouths to feed every day as I would for an entire dinner party! My mum told me of times when an unexpected guest would drop in, and her mother would always find a way to feed one more person.

This reminds me of the story of the two fish and five loaves of bread. One Sunday my pastor asked us to consider: *What if it weren't a divine miracle, but a human miracle?* The scripture only describes how the miracle was performed – the bread and fish were blessed, broken and shared with those seated. But could it be that by divine example people shared with others the food they had brought for their journey?

If on that day people came together to feed a multitude, can't we find the generosity to include one more at each meal? For most of us, giving such a small donation is possible. For others, receiving such a meal may be a miracle of great magnitude.

Prayer: *Dear Lord, thank you for our daily bread. Give us the opportunity and also the courage to feed one more. Amen*

Thought for the day: How can I share my abundance with those in my community?

Macie Craven (Oklahoma, USA)

Unexpected

Read Mark 10:35–45

'This will be a sign for you: you will find a child wrapped in bands of cloth and lying in a manger.'
Luke 2:12 (NRSV)

For a year my sister, Chinwe, and I had excitedly planned her son's destination wedding. Three days before the wedding, I flew from Lagos to Puerto Vallarta, Mexico, with decorations for the colourful Nigerian ceremony. But then we had a shock. Chinwe was hospitalised, getting tested for kidney stones. If the tests were positive, she would need urgent surgery. Thanks be to God, the tests were negative.

We can never anticipate what will happen. I wonder if Mary expected her long, dusty journey to Bethlehem or the rejection of the innkeeper. Did she know her beloved baby – the eternal king – would have to lie in a manger? Similarly, the apostles in Mark 10 expected Jesus to have an earthly throne and wanted to sit beside him. They didn't anticipate their modest lives or the suffering they would experience.

Disappointments dot our lives – failed business ventures, broken relationships, lost loved ones, rejected job applications, unanswered prayers. When things do not go as we expect, we can learn to trust the eternal king, who was born in a stable. God is always with us.

Prayer: *Loving Father, increase our faith and trust that you will see us through every disappointment. Amen*

Thought for the day: In every unexpected event, I will look for God's presence.

Nenye Andy-Eke (Lagos, Nigeria)

My old bird feeder

Read Matthew 6:25–34

Look at the birds of the air; they neither sow nor reap nor gather into barns, and yet your heavenly Father feeds them. Are you not of more value than they?

Matthew 6:26 (NRSV)

I looked out into the backyard and smiled at the sight of the old bird feeder dangling from its hook. A handful of seeds remained from the winter, and the sound of birds echoed in the distance. My thoughts drifted back to the day I bought that feeder.

Back then, my pay cheque was far less than I had hoped – the result of a poor quarter in company sales and a near miss on a performance bonus. The medical bills from a growing family and a season of difficulty presented fears I hadn't imagined as I calculated how little might remain after paying the bills. In the day that followed, my Bible study time ended with the words from today's reading, 'Look at the birds of the air; they do not sow or reap or store away in barns, and yet your heavenly Father feeds them. Are you not much more valuable than they?' (NIV). The words were timely, and I made up my mind to do two things: tithe before paying a single bill and buy a bird feeder.

Now, years later, when times feel tough and uncertainty or trouble looms near, the bird feeder reminds me that I am more valuable than the birds that God feeds and cares for every day.

Prayer: *Dear God, when uncertainties cause us to worry, help us to seek you first and to trust with joy and hope that you will give us what we need. Amen*

Thought for the day: What helps me to trust in God's provision?

Cassius Rhue (South Carolina, USA)

The visitor

Read Matthew 5:14–16
Let each of you look not to your own interests, but to the interests of others.
Philippians 2:4 (NRSV)

Our home church recently decided to become a friendlier place for visitors. As a result, one of our members saw a man on his own whom she did not recognise, began a conversation with him and introduced him to her circle of friends. This hospitality took some courage from our member, who normally only chats with those she knows. But when it was time to leave, the visitor said to her, 'I came to church today feeling quite lonely and lost. I was so relieved when you started to talk to me. You have been my angel today.' How good is that! This woman spread the love of Jesus by making the visitor feel valued and loved through simple conversation.

I believe Christians and churches should be the friendliest people and places on earth, but often we are not that welcoming. We tend to sit with our family and friends during the church services and mostly talk with those we know afterward. However, when we commit to welcoming new people and sharing the love we have experienced in Christ, we can show others that they are loved and valued by God.

Prayer: *Dear Lord, help us to value others, especially strangers. May we show people your love by the way we value them. Amen*

Thought for the day: I can share God's love through simple conversation.

Irene Robinson (Gauteng, South Africa)

Third Sunday of Advent

Read John 1:1–14

Unto you is born this day in the city of David a Saviour, which is Christ the Lord.
Luke 2:11 (KJV)

When I visited New York City during the holiday season, I stopped by the Christmas tree at Rockefeller Center. It was over 70 feet tall and looked spectacular with thousands of lights and a bright star. I was delighted by the sounds of families and friends enjoying the festivities together. Even strangers jovially greeted one another with a wave while holding hot coffee and cocoa.

Christmastime is wonderful, and I enjoy it every year. But if I didn't know the true meaning of Christmas, my joy would be as temporary as the tree displayed each year at Rockefeller Center. When the holidays are over, the tree is taken away and so are the special greetings of the season. But praise God that the good tidings of great joy given that first Christmas remain always! My happiness during the holiday season is fleeting, but my joy in Jesus is eternal.

The story of Christmas is one of salvation and redemption. Jesus Christ, the Son of God, came into the world to redeem us and to restore our relationship with God, and that story keeps me awestruck all year long.

Prayer: *Heavenly Father, thank you for the gift of your Son, Jesus, and for our everlasting joy in him. Amen*

Thought for the day: I can find joy in Jesus all year long.

Aaron Caruso (Connecticut, USA)

Come to me

Read Isaiah 55:1–3

Why spend money on what is not bread, and your labour on what does not satisfy?
Isaiah 55:2 (NIV)

Tap, tap, tap! *What is making that noise?* I wondered. Upon investigation, I discovered a persistent little woodpecker tapping on a metal light pole where he would never find an insect for breakfast.

Pondering this curious sight, I thought about how often we humans go after false sources of nourishment, like popularity, money, education or success. Jesus tells us, 'I am the bread of life. Whoever comes to me will never go hungry, and whoever believes in me will never be thirsty' (John 6:35). Jesus is the source of abundant life! Only he can satisfy our hunger. We are hungry and thirsty, seeking sustenance from false sources like a woodpecker on a metal pole. But when we listen to Jesus' call 'Come to me!' and open ourselves to God's word, we can receive new life (see John 7:37).

Prayer: *Father God, help us to hear your call and respond so that we can share your love with others. We pray the prayer your Son taught us, 'Our Father which art in heaven, hallowed be thy name. Thy kingdom come, thy will be done in earth, as it is in heaven. Give us this day our daily bread. And forgive us our debts, as we forgive our debtors. And lead us not into temptation, but deliver us from evil: For thine is the kingdom, and the power, and the glory, for ever. Amen.'**

Thought for the day: Jesus is the true nourishment I need.

Glenda (Revell) Paquette (Ontario, Canada)

God knows what we need

Read Psalm 103:13–18

The Lord is close to the broken-hearted and saves those who are crushed in spirit.

Psalm 34:18 (NIV)

I attended a worship service in my church with a heavy heart. My dad was dying, and nothing more could be done for him medically. Tears streamed down my face, but I could not easily leave because I was sitting in the front row where I expected a friend to join me. Beautiful flowers rested on the altar table and the sermon was inspiring. But what touched me most that day were the hymns we sang with joy and enthusiasm. Those hymns touched my heart and reminded me that God knows exactly what we need.

When the service was over, my face was tear-stained. But I left the church feeling far better than when I entered. I knew that whatever lay ahead for my dad and me, my heavenly Father would give me strength. I resolved to keep my heart receptive to the experiences God offers me and the ways God wants me to use my life.

My dad is now with my mother in heaven. And God is still faithful. I give thanks that God is always available to us in our pain and in our joy.

Prayer: *Good and gracious God, help us to remember that your grace is sufficient for our every need. May our focus be on you always. We pray in the name of your Son, Jesus. Amen*

Thought for the day: When my heart is heavy, spending time with God can lighten the burden.

Judith Wolfgang (Kentucky, USA)

PRAYER FOCUS: SOMEONE WHOSE PARENT IS DYING

The news is good

Read Matthew 11:25–30

'Come to me, all you that are weary and are carrying heavy burdens, and I will give you rest.'
Matthew 11:28 (NRSV)

Every Christmas, my wife brings out a tattered recipe for Christmas pudding that she has made for almost four decades. She inherited the recipe, which my mother made for her family each Christmas. The much-loved recipe is faded, smudged and stained. Yet it brings joy to our family every year.

By the time I reach the Christmas season at the end of the year, my heart is also tattered. Whatever joy I held at the beginning of the year has faded. The clarity of my vision is smudged. I am stained by let-downs, setbacks and defeats.

That's when I know it is time to bring out the well-loved story of the angel announcing Jesus' birth in Luke 2. The angel announcing the birth of Christ our Saviour brings joy to our expectant hearts. After a hard year of challenge, stress and struggle, this is truly good news of great joy! God has never forgotten us and comes to renew us each year at Christmastime.

Prayer: *Gracious God, after a hard year help us to remember the good news of Christ our Saviour. May we discover in him the fullness of your joy. Amen*

Thought for the day: The season's news is good – Christ is born to us!

Graham N. West (Wisconsin, USA)

Faith in action

Read Romans 12:9–13

John answered, 'Anyone who has two shirts should share with the one who has none, and anyone who has food should do the same.'
Luke 3:11 (NIV)

My friend and I sat under a tree during our lunch break. As we began to open our lunch boxes, we noticed a girl from our class sitting under another tree without anything to eat. So we went and shared our lunches with her. The following day, we noticed that she did not have food again. We asked her why, and she told us that her mother was sick with typhoid and could not make lunch for her. For the next few days, my friend insisted that we share our food.

My friend's determination to share her food reminded me of Jesus' feeding the 5,000 in the gospel of John when Jesus blessed a young boy's lunch so that he could feed the crowd. When others expressed doubts that everyone could be fed, Andrew went among the crowd to see what food was available. Small acts made a tremendous difference that day. In a similar way, my friend saw a need and acted with compassion and love.

In a world where acts of selfless love are rare, followers of Jesus are called to put the interests of others above our own. The Christian life is a life of faith and works. If we are followers of Christ, we must show our faith in action by reaching out to those who are in need.

Prayer: *Loving God, help us to be mindful of those who are oppressed and marginalised in our society. Grant us the kindness and courage to love them as Christ loves us. Amen*

Thought for the day: I can demonstrate my faith by sharing what I have with those in need.

Navamani Peter (Karnataka, India)

A simple note

Read 1 Thessalonians 5:9–15

Therefore encourage one another and build each other up, just as in fact you are doing.
1 Thessalonians 5:11 (NIV)

Part of my job is introducing new computer software to travel agencies across the country. One software package was particularly complicated, and Emily, the training manager, was nervous about teaching it to our clients. Emily ended up doing a great job, so I wanted to show my appreciation. I wrote her a note of thanks for her help and good work.

Two weeks later a handwritten letter from Emily arrived on my desk. Part of that note has remained clear in my mind: 'I've worked here for over 15 years and no one has ever written me a personal note of appreciation like this. I was having a really bad day when your letter arrived, and it just picked me right up. You have no idea how much this means to me.'

I put the letter down, feeling humbled and thinking, *How could a handwritten note that took me just a few minutes to write make such a big impact?* And then I wondered why I wasn't doing this more often if it could make such a difference.

Today's reading from 1 Thessalonians urges us to encourage one another. It can be difficult to know when someone is struggling or needing encouragement. This exchange of thank-you notes showed me how even a small gesture of care can show God's love.

Prayer: *Dear Lord, show us the people who need our encouragement so that we can share your love through our small acts of kindness today and every day. Amen*

Thought for the day: Through my simple words of encouragement, God can change lives.

Tom Smith (Utah, USA)

The Lord is our refuge

Read Matthew 15:21–28

If you say, 'The Lord is my refuge,' and you make the Most High your dwelling, no harm will overtake you, no disaster will come near your tent. For he will command his angels concerning you to guard you in all your ways.

Psalm 91:9–11 (NIV)

When my daughter left to study in another city, I was alone for the first time in my life. This was a big transition for me. I had grown used to caring for my daughter and teaching her. We spent almost all our time together. It was difficult to let her go, but it was necessary. This is the normal course of life. In contrast, my daughter, filled with hopes, dreams and excitement, was happy for her independence.

As a Christian parent, I find great comfort in prayer. Every day I trust my daughter's life into God's hands and ask God to provide her protection and wisdom. Even though my daughter is now an adult and living in another city, prayer is one way that I can continue to care for her every day and night. I have found that prayer also gives me strength and helps me adjust to a new stage in my life.

Prayer: *Dear God, we are grateful that we can trust our loved ones to your care. We ask you to protect and bless them every day. Amen*

Thought for the day: My prayers sustain my loved ones and strengthen me.

Andra Laum (Saaremaa, Estonia)

Fourth Sunday of Advent

Read Luke 1:26–38
'Nothing is impossible for God.'
Luke 1:37 (CEB)

It's impossible. Surely this thought went through Mary's mind as the angel revealed God's plan. But then the heavenly messenger went on to prove his authenticity by informing Mary of another impossibility happening to her cousin Elizabeth, who was far past the age of childbearing but was in her sixth month of pregnancy. From a biological perspective, there was no good reason for why these things should come to pass. But they revealed the divine truth spoken by the angel: 'Nothing is impossible for God.'

Taking a closer look at this story, I've noticed there are three elements leading up to the impossible being made possible. The scripture points out that Mary was humble. Second, she was enabled by the power of the Most High; the impossible was not her doing. Lastly, she believed God's promise and trusted that it would be as the angel said.

So the next time the Lord asks us to do something seemingly impossible, we don't need to fear. Following Mary's example, we can humbly let our creator's power work through us and trust God's faithfulness. The Almighty delights in working with us, in us and through us to accomplish the impossible.

Prayer: *Dear Father, help us to follow Mary's example and trust in you. Use us to accomplish your purposes – even when it seems impossible to us. Amen*

Thought for the day: Everything is possible for God.

Joe Di Francesco (Ontario, Canada)

A God who forgives

Read Ephesians 1:3–10

If anyone is in Christ, the new creation has come: the old has gone, the new is here!
2 Corinthians 5:17 (NIV)

My little sister and I love to play rough. Even though our rowdiness can annoy our family, it's all in good fun and no one gets seriously hurt – usually. This pattern broke recently when my sister's heel collided with the top of my pointer finger as we were wrestling. By the next morning, my finger was swollen, purple and stiff. I saw this as an opportunity to make my sister feel guilty. Throughout the day, I jokingly told my sister, 'You have to do what I ask you to do, because you broke my finger.'

My sister knew I was just teasing her, but my actions made me think about how differently Jesus responds to our mistakes. Jesus doesn't use our mistakes against us to make us feel guilty. Rather, his love overcomes our failures. Because he died on the cross, we all have a clean slate. Jesus forgives us.

God will never hold our shortcomings against us. In Christ, we are free from guilt. In Christ, we are holy, good and redeemed.

Prayer: *Dear Jesus, thank you for the way that you love us. Help us to live into our new identity in you. Amen*

Thought for the day: Thanks to Christ's grace, my past mistakes do not define me.

Savannah Yokel (Alabama, USA)

At the feet of Christ

Read Luke 10:38–42

'Very truly I tell you, whoever believes in me will do the works I have been doing, and they will do even greater things than these, because I am going to the Father.'
John 14:12 (NIV)

When I think about the struggle for women's rights around the world, I am reminded of the women who came before me. They overcame many challenges, and their work allows me to be where I am. I especially think of the time many of those women must have spent at the feet of Jesus.

In Luke 10, Mary sat at Jesus' feet to hear his teachings. Women did not often participate in teaching this way, but Mary overcame prejudice to listen to Jesus. Like Mary, my mother always overcame challenges to spend time with Christ. She valued daily family devotional time, and she always made time for us to share our experiences and pray. My paternal grandmother also had a strong faith, and she regularly recited Bible verses to express it. She worked tirelessly to support her children, staying strong and overcoming challenges.

John 14:12 makes me reflect on the great works of so many women – works that reached far beyond their own lives. May we be grateful to those who have inspired our faith and paved the way for us. And may the image of sitting at Jesus' feet lead us to reflect on the ways we can overcome difficulties and do great works.

Prayer: *Dear God, thank you for the women who inspire us. Help us as we navigate life's challenges while striving to stay near to you. In the name of Jesus. Amen*

Thought for the day: Because of my faith, I can do great works and inspire the faith of others.

Beatriz Nascimento (Rio de Janeiro, Brazil)

The power of presence

Read Mark 14:32–42

[Jesus] said to them, 'I'm very sad. It's as if I'm dying. Stay here and keep alert.'
Mark 14:34 (CEB)

When I became a pastor at 22, I lived in fear of having to perform the sacred duty of saying final words at a graveside service. I didn't know what I would say or do.

On my first day as a pastor, Hill, a 70-year-old seasoned church leader, told me, 'You're our pastor. Tell us what to do, and we'll follow.' His trust gave me courage to lead. But after only two months, Hill's wife, Alma, called to tell me that Hill had died. In the face of his loss, I felt unable to do anything useful for Alma or the church.

As funeral arrangements were made over the next two days, I said a few words and prayers. But mostly I just sat with Alma, held her hand and shared her grief. Alma told me she couldn't have gotten through it without me. It wasn't eloquent words or grand gestures that made a difference; it was presence.

God came in the person of Jesus to be present with us. But we can get so busy trying to be useful that we forget to be present with God. As we prepare to celebrate Christ's birth, let us not forget to spend sacred time sitting quietly and soaking in the presence of Emmanuel.

Prayer: *Dear Lord, in the hustle and bustle of our days, help us to be intentionally present so that we can connect with you and with those around us. Amen*

Thought for the day: My presence can remind others of the presence of Christ.

Kevin Thomas (Alabama, USA)

Cheerful giver

Read 2 Corinthians 9:5–10

Each of you must give as you have made up your mind, not reluctantly or under compulsion, for God loves a cheerful giver.
2 Corinthians 9:7 (NRSV)

While on holiday with our four children, we were eating at a family restaurant. Our six-year-old, Jon, noticed the chocolate bars below the counter by the cash register. He had put his earnings from helping around the house in his pocket 'just in case', so after dinner, Jon wandered towards the confectionary. Glancing over, I noticed he was conversing at length with our server.

Returning to the table, Jon proudly displayed three giant packages of peanut butter cups with four cups each. I felt a little disappointed. I had hoped he would spend his money on a souvenir from the trip instead – something more lasting than confectionary. Laying the three packages on the table he said, 'I did the math, and I bought three packs so that each of us can have two!' He smiled broadly, excited by his plan. He was not 'wasting' all of his money on chocolate, as I had thought. He was using his money to give us all a treat.

God wants us to be like Jon. Our creator wants us to look beyond ourselves when we have abundance, 'doing the math' so that we can share our wealth. The joy that we gain in sharing our gifts is a part of the gift itself.

Prayer: *Dear God, show us ways that we can be cheerful givers. Empower us to think beyond ourselves and share what we have with others. Amen*

Thought for the day: I will share a gift with someone today.

Jesse Jeanne Neve (Minnesota, USA)

The light of God

Read Genesis 1:1–5
Without faith it is impossible to please God.
Hebrews 11:6 (NIV)

I oversee a church programme that teaches people the art of solar cooking. On one memorable mission trip, we were scheduled to leave early in the morning because the mission site was far from where we spent the night. It had rained quite a bit the previous night. Our spirits were low as we worried about having enough sunlight to teach properly that day.

Early in the morning as I walked to the main road to guide our driver back to where the rest of the group was waiting, I noticed a woman spreading clean laundry out to dry. The faith of that woman buoyed my spirit and inspired hope. She could not know for certain that the sun would shine to dry her laundry, but her action reminded me of Hebrews 11:1: 'Faith is confidence in what we hope for and assurance about what we do not see.'

There will be times when it feels like it has been raining all night, that daylight will never come and the sun will not shine. But we can turn to our faith and the words of scripture for reassurance that no matter how long and dark the night has been, the sun will shine again.

Prayer: *Eternal God, when our hopes are low, give us courage to persevere and faith to trust in the light of your love. In the name of Jesus we pray. Amen*

Thought for the day: For those who wait on the Lord, the light of God will shine brightly.

Erasme Figaro (Dominican Republic)

God is with us

Read Matthew 1:18–25

'The virgin will conceive and give birth to a son, and they will call him Immanuel' (which means 'God with us').
Matthew 1:23 (NIV)

As worship leader in my church, I always planned the Christmas worship services with great care and excitement. One year I asked a soprano named Rebecca to sing 'O Holy Night' during the last Sunday morning service before Christmas.

As the date approached, Rebecca called me and said, 'I keep feeling like God wants me to sing 'O Holy Night' in French. Is that weird?' I told her I thought it would be glorious, and that if God was leading her to do it, then she should. Our church had an English-speaking international congregation with 15 countries represented weekly. We were not aware of any attendees from French-speaking countries, but we both felt certain this was God's plan. We had no idea just how beautiful God's plan was.

That week in our Sunday service, a French businessman was depressed because he had to spend the holidays far from home. He was feeling discouraged and alone until Rebecca sang. As he listened to the hymn, he was flooded with the love of God and knew he was not alone. God encouraged and blessed that man through our simple act of obedience. That Christmas will forever remind me that Jesus truly is Immanuel, God with us.

Prayer: *Dear Lord God, thank you for blessing us as your children. Remind those who feel alone that you are with them. Amen*

Thought for the day: God is with us always.

Terrie Hellard-Brown (Oklahoma, USA)

Christmas Day

Read Luke 2:8–14

Suddenly a great assembly of the heavenly forces was with the angel praising God.
Luke 2:13 (CEB)

As a young girl, I found the Christmas season to be tremendously exciting. It was a season for singing and celebrating. And almost everyone in the village would buy new clothes. The Christmas spirit could be felt all around, especially at church in the sounds of singing and drumming. Everybody in the village knew Christmas was a time to eat the best meals. Even those who could not afford to buy meat any other time of the year would make sure they had some for Christmas. On Christmas day the singing, the clapping of hands and the drumming seemed to join with the heavenly host in praising God.

I imagine that there was no less excitement when the angel of the Lord appeared to the shepherds in the field who were watching over their sheep. After the angel had told them the good news of the birth of Christ, there appeared a multitude of angels praising God!

In this Christmas season, let us join in singing – for Christ is born! Let us also announce the good news of his birth all around us so that others can come and celebrate the joy of Christmas with us.

Prayer: *Dear Lord, may the joy of Christmas fill our hearts as we offer our praise to you. In Jesus' name. Amen*

Thought for the day: Christmas is a time to celebrate the good news of Christ Jesus.

Enid Adah Nyinomujuni (Dar es Salaam, Tanzania)

Preparing the altar

Read Matthew 25:14–30

Each of you should use whatever gift you have received to serve others, as faithful stewards of God's grace in its various forms.
1 Peter 4:10 (NIV)

For several years it has been my responsibility and joy to prepare my church's altar for the Sunday morning worship service. Rather than use traditional floral arrangements, I draw inspiration from the lectionary and sermon topic for the coming Sunday. Through prayer and the Holy Spirit, I transform the altar into a visual expression of scripture and the pastor's message. On several occasions I've been frustrated when I had to start over because my original plan did not work out. But the final offering has always been meaningful and appreciated by our congregation.

Preparing the altar each Sunday has blessed me in many ways: scriptures have taken on new meaning, sermons have come alive and I've developed a keener appreciation for common objects that can be transformed into meaningful symbols. My hope is always that the altar will add yet another layer of meaning to the worship experience. For a long time I didn't know how to respond when people commented on the altar presentation, but I now tell them it's the ministry that God has granted me. I've been the beneficiary of true blessings while serving in this capacity.

Prayer: *Generous God, help us to discover and use the special gifts you have given us. Amen*

Thought for the day: Serving God connects me more deeply to my faith.

Stanley Hartness (Mississippi, USA)

An angel in the garden

Read Luke 24:1-8

Suddenly two men in clothes that gleamed like lightning stood beside them. In their fright the women bowed down with their faces to the ground, but the men said to them, 'Why do you look for the living among the dead?'
Luke 24:4-5 (NIV)

Last winter on a bright December's day, I hung out the washing in the garden to dry. The sharp sun threw light on to a metallic bird feeder which cast reflected rays of light on to the garden fence. The light darted back and forth as the gusts of wind moved the feeder. It looked like an angel had entered our garden.

There are many incidents in the Bible where people meet with angels, most notably around the birth of Jesus. Perhaps because I was in a garden and the light so bright, my thoughts turned to Mary Magdalene and the other women who went to the garden where Jesus was buried. The stone had been rolled away from the tomb, so that they were able to enter, but the tomb was empty. Suddenly two men in bright shining clothes appeared to them with the message that Jesus had been raised. Just as angels announced Jesus' birth, now they also announced his resurrection.

I gave thanks to God that this simple reflection of sunlight in the middle of winter reminded me of the good news of the risen Jesus!

Prayer: *Dear Father, thank you that, as the psalmist declares, all of creation declares your glory. Amen*

Thought for the day: I will reflect the light of the risen Christ to those around me today.

Faith Ford (England, United Kingdom)

All of creation

Read Psalm 104:24–30

How many are your works, Lord! In wisdom you made them all; the earth is full of your creatures.
Psalm 104:24 (NIV)

My mother has a small garden in our backyard where she grows several kinds of flowering plants. One particular plant with purple flowers stands out from the rest. Every morning, the plant displays beautiful flowers that face up towards the sky. But by noon, the flowers have all withered and fallen off, one by one. At night we can find no new flowers among the leaves. But by the next morning, fresh purple flowers appear again.

I am amazed at how God perfectly takes care of each and every part of creation. When I consider all the living things on this earth, I recognise that my mother's purple flowers are a very small part of creation. Yet God never fails to bring up new flowers each morning after the previous ones have fallen off.

There are billions of people and innumerable living things, each with specific needs. Yet God cares for each part of creation. I believe God hears all our prayers and praises, and God works to bring us good things.

Prayer: *O God, we are grateful for your creation. Thank you for the goodness and care you provide for every living thing. Amen*

Thought for the day: Even though I am a small part of God's creation, God cares deeply for me.

Juita Kartini (Jakarta, Indonesia)

Jesus' compassion

Read Luke 7:1–10

Just then there came a man named Jairus, a leader of the synagogue. He fell at Jesus' feet and begged him to come to his house, for he had an only daughter, about twelve years old, who was dying.
Luke 8:41–42 (NRSV)

In the gospel of Luke, Jairus, a leader of the synagogue, begged Jesus to come heal his very sick daughter (see Luke 8:40–56). Jairus demonstrated great faith, believing that Jesus could heal his daughter simply by laying his hands on her. Jesus honoured his faith by agreeing to follow him to his home.

However, prior to this meeting, Jesus had an encounter with a centurion who interceded for his servant's healing. But instead of allowing Jesus to come lay his hands on his servant, the centurion asked that Jesus simply say the word and his servant would be healed. He recognised that Jesus' word was as good as his presence. The centurion's faith amazed me.

I find it comforting that Jesus had the same compassion for Jairus even though he asked for healing in a different way than the centurion had. It is indeed an encouragement to know that Jesus will have compassion on us wherever our needs draw him. Jesus will not reject us but will meet us where we are. While it is good to learn from the faith of others, we can be confident that no matter our circumstance, trial or need, Jesus will never forsake us.

Prayer: *Compassionate God, thank you for loving each of us just the way we are and for judging us not by the expression of our faith but by the depth of your mercy. Amen*

Thought for the day: Jesus will show compassion to me no matter what.

Benjamin Wayo (Federal Capital Territory, Nigeria)

Our shield

Read Psalm 3
You, Lord, are a shield around me, my glory, the One who lifts my head high.
Psalm 3:3 (NIV)

Years ago, my family moved to Mozambique to do mission work. The poverty we witnessed often broke our hearts, but singing with our neighbours in church always moved us from worry to faith and trust. One of my favourite worship songs that we learned from our Mozambican friends translates to something like 'Daniel prayed to God, and the lions licked him.' In the song's original language, the rhythm is energising and the catchy tune always encourages singing and dancing.

The song invites us to celebrate the power of God that can shut the lion's mouth. As the psalmist writes, God is our shield and defender, the lifter of our heads. When we focus on our creator's power, our worries are put in perspective.

Being in communion with God in worship is one way to stay focused on our creator despite the troubles we face. When I sing in church, I see myself as a little girl and God as my loving parent who lifts my head high. I gaze into my creator's eyes and trust that nothing can harm me as long as I am surrounded by God, my shield.

Prayer: *Dear God, help us to stay focused on you in a world full of worries. Amen*

Thought for the day: Worship can move me from worry to peace.

Susan E. Brooks (Kentucky, USA)

Renew our strength

Read 1 Samuel 30:1–6

David strengthened himself in the Lord his God.
1 Samuel 30:6 (NRSV)

In January 2020, our city faced the biggest flood in its history. A newly renovated church in the community had just invested in quality equipment and furniture, but floodwaters hit the facilities and caused many material losses. I had been a pastor in the community for twelve years, and my heart ached when I witnessed the chaotic aftermath.

In moments like this, we become plagued by frustration, anguish and discouragement. But the word of God meets us in adversity and strengthens us. In 1 Samuel 30, we read about David's intense reaction to Ziklag's destruction. He wept and grieved but did not allow his anguish to overwhelm him. David's faith in God revived his strength. He sought God's guidance and in due course retrieved everything that had been taken. This testimony inspired me and the members of the church, reviving our strength so we could move forward and start over.

We all live through difficult moments, and in such times dejection often tries to settle in our hearts. But like David, we can revive our strength in God. Let us always pray and carry on, for in God's timing we will surely find renewal.

Prayer: *Dear Lord, in the face of adversity, we place our hope in you. Revive us in the name of Jesus. Amen*

Thought for the day: I will face adversity with faith and perseverance, trusting that God will help me through.

Márcio Abreu de Freitas (Brazil)

Small group questions

Wednesday 7 September

1 Have you ever attended a spiritual retreat? What was your experience? How did you integrate what you learned into your daily life? If you have not attended a spiritual retreat, what do you think you might gain from one?

2 Describe a time when you worried that distance would affect your ability to connect with someone. How were you able to overcome the obstacle of physical distance in your relationship with this person?

3 Have you ever participated in virtual worship or Bible study? Did you feel the Lord's presence in those experiences? Name some ways virtual fellowship differs from in-person fellowship. What challenges does it create? What opportunities?

4 How can meeting regularly with another Christian to study scripture, books and hymns enrich your faith? Where do you find community with other Christians?

5 In what ways is your faith strengthened by the faith of others? What do you find most powerful about God's design for faith in community?

Wednesday 14 September

1 Today's writer describes feeling numb after the death of her brother. When have you felt numb? How did your numbness change the ways you interacted with the world and with God?

2 Do you find it easy or difficult to connect with God through physical exercise? What activities and locations best help you to feel God's presence?

3 When have your usual ways of interacting with God felt stale or hollow? How do you reconnect with God when you feel unmoored and alone?

4 When have you felt Jesus weeping with you? How did his presence help you process your sadness and grief? In what other ways did you experience God's healing and understanding?

5 What advice would you offer someone who is seeking to reconnect with God? How can you come alongside someone and support them in their journey back to God?

Wednesday 21 September

1 Explain a spiritual lesson you have learned from a piece of secular music, art or literature. How did this spiritual insight change the way you experience the piece?

2 When have you neglected a gift? When has someone neglected a gift that you gave them? Did they ever come to appreciate the gift? What did you learn from this experience?

3 Describe the moment you opened God's gift of salvation. How did you feel? What changes did you experience in yourself and in your life?

4 Name three reasons someone may not open the gift of salvation. What emotional, spiritual or physical help can you offer others to encourage them to open the gift?

5 How do you express your gratitude to God through service? In what other ways do you express your gratitude to God? How do your acts of gratitude bring abundance to your life?

Wednesday 28 September

1 What scene in the Bible can you imagine most vividly? Why that scene? How does it impact you?

2 Do you find it easy or difficult to look past all that divides us and to love all people? Why? What verses, prayers and spiritual practices help you when you are focused on our divisions?

3 How does Jesus' humility change the way you live? In what ways does Jesus' example help you to love and serve others with humility? Who else in the Bible exemplifies humility and love?

4 Is it possible to love others selfishly? Why or why not? How do you keep your love for others selfless and focused on Jesus? What happens if your focus strays from Jesus?

5 How does your faith community help you to follow God's guidance as you spread the love of Christ? What changes do you see in yourself, in your community and in those you serve when you serve out of selfless love?

Wednesday 5 October

1 Have you ever rejected an answer to prayer hoping that something better might come along? Did you regret your choice? What was the outcome of your situation?

2 Have you ever viewed yourself as a failure when circumstances didn't go the way you had hoped? What did this experience teach you about failure and the way that God looks at us when we don't succeed?

3 Describe a time when you found a scripture passage that spoke to you. Why did you relate to the scripture so deeply?

4 Name some people in the Bible who did not receive the answer to prayer that they had hoped for. Which of these stories is most helpful for you? Why?

5 How does it encourage you to know that God is always making things new? How does your faith community remind you to always look towards the new things God is doing?

Wednesday 12 October

1 Why do you think we tend to place more value on the work of those who are on the frontlines than that of those who are behind the scenes? How can you be more intentional about recognising and appreciating the contributions of those working behind the scenes?

2 Do you prefer to be in the background or front-and-centre? Why? How do you think other people view your contributions?

3 Who in the Bible worked behind the scenes to help spread the good news about Christ? Do you think Christ's message would have spread as far as it has without their efforts? Why or why not?

4 Do you ever find yourself considering some roles in God's kingdom more important than others? Why? What scripture verses remind you that every role is essential?

5 What is your role in God's kingdom? How do you know that this is your role? What advice and encouragement do you have for someone who is unsure of their role?

Wednesday 19 October

1 What in nature do you view as a symbol of God's grace? Why is it a helpful image for you?

2 The tree in today's meditation sprouted up without being planted. When have you witnessed something spontaneous that ended up being a blessing to many? How do the results of spontaneous gifts differ from those that are planned and intentional?

3 What images of God's grace do you see around you? Do you seek out those images or do you find them without effort? How do those images inform your faith and actions?

4 Are we able to truly know and understand God's grace? Why or why not? How do scripture, Christian community and nature bring you closer to understanding grace?

5   In what ways can you extend a bit of God's grace to someone today?
    In what ways are others extending God's grace to you?

Wednesday 26 October

1   Do you tend to see the big picture or do you focus on the details?
    Why is it sometimes easier to focus on one more than the other?

2   When have you felt that you were out of place in life? What made
    you feel this way? What helps remind you that you fit perfectly
    into God's plan? When are you most confident in your place in
    God's kingdom?

3   How do we discover God's will for our life? How can we be sure that
    we are following God's will for us?

4   Do you find it easy or difficult to accept God's will? Do you ever
    wish God would change your situation? What scripture verses and
    prayers help you find peace and accept that God's plans for you are
    better than your own?

5   How do you remain faithful and trust that you fit perfectly into
    God's plan? How does your faith community help you to stay
    the course?

Wednesday 2 November

1   When you observe a need in your community, do you take action or
    do you wait for someone else to? Why?

2   Have you ever felt that you were the wrong age or in the wrong
    season of life to answer a call from God? How can you combat those
    feelings? How are you encouraged by Abraham's example of serving
    God regardless of his age?

3   When you doubt that you will be able to bless others, what scripture
    passages remind you that God can use anyone at any time?

4 When you feel a call from God to serve, what is your first response? Where do you find the strength to answer the call? What happens when you do?

5 Who in your community has blessed you with their service? How will you let them know you appreciate their actions?

Wednesday 9 November

1 Have you ever used a specific method for memorising scripture? If so, what was the experience like? If not, how do you choose which Bible verses you will memorise?

2 When do you most clearly experience the power of God's word? In what ways does scripture bring you peace and encourage you to worship?

3 Describe a time when scripture has offered you comfort or a sense of healing. Why was God's word so beneficial for you in that time? What else brought you healing?

4 What spiritual disciplines have most enriched your faith? How have they enriched your faith? What other spiritual disciplines would you like to try?

5 Can worship and worry inhabit you at the same time? Explain. When you are filled with worry, what forms of worship help to shift your focus?

Wednesday 16 November

1 When it is time to prepare for the holidays, what is your job? How did you end up with this role? Describe a time when you saw your contribution bring joy to someone else.

2 Name three ways that the gifts of people in your church enrich your life. How do you embrace your own gifts and share them with others in your community?

3   When you believe that your gifts are inadequate, what prayers and forms of worship help you to see their value?

4   Do you find joy in sharing your gifts with those around you? If so, where does that joy come from?

5   Do you possess a gift that you are hesitant to share? Why are you hesitant? How does scripture encourage you to share your gift with confidence?

Wednesday 23 November

1   Describe something that you have seen recently that seems to have been forgotten. What did you think when you saw it? Where were you at the time? What about it indicated that it had been forgotten?

2   Why do you think it is so easy for the world to forget people? In what ways do you try to avoid forgetting someone? How do you help those whom others seem to have forgotten?

3   When has someone's actions shown you that you are not forgotten? How did those actions affect you? How does this experience inspire you to show others that they are not forgotten?

4   What can you learn from Jesus' example of noticing those whom society had dismissed? How can Christians better live like Jesus did when it comes to people who have been neglected by the world?

5   When have you witnessed small actions make a big difference for an individual or for a group of people? What did that situation teach you about your role in helping others and the difference that you can make?

Wednesday 30 November

1   Have you always celebrated Christmas? Why or why not? How has the way you observe Christmas changed throughout your life?

2   How has the meaning of Christmas changed for you throughout the years?

3 What does the celebration of Christmas mean to you? What feelings towards God and others does the Christmas season bring out most strongly for you?

4 How do you share the good news of Christ's birth with those around you at Christmastime?

5 In what ways does your faith community encourage you to celebrate and give thanks in the Christmas season? What gifts from God do you and your church most clearly focus on and celebrate?

Wednesday 7 December

1 Have you ever had unexpected guests show up at mealtime? What did you do? After this experience, how did this change the way you planned for and prepared meals?

2 Do you think the feeding of the 5,000 was a divine miracle or a human one? Could it be both? How would your understanding of the story change depending on which you think it is?

3 When have you observed an act of generosity that inspired another generous act? In what ways did it encourage you to live more generously each day?

4 When have you been on the receiving end of a donation that made all the difference for you? In what ways did that miracle of generosity change your situation? How did you respond?

5 How will you share generously with others this season? What might it look like to include one more person at each meal? What difference do you want to make in the lives of others?

Wednesday 14 December

1 Does your family have a treasured recipe or tradition this time of year? Why do you think we pass recipes and traditions down through the generations?

2 How do you relate to the writer's experience of having a tattered and worn heart by the end of each year? What brings you renewal when those feelings arise?

3 What Bible stories or faith traditions help you and your family reconnect with God in the Christmas season? How do you reconnect with God other times of the year?

4 Does this time of year bring you renewal like it does for today's writer? Why or why not? Name specific ways you will seek God's renewing love this season.

5 After a difficult year, is it easier or harder for you to remember the good news of Christ? Why? In what ways does your church community help you remember the good news and find peace?

Wednesday 21 December

1 Has your church ever lost a beloved leader? How did that loss change your church? Where did the congregation find strength during this time?

2 When has someone's trust in you given you the confidence to move forward? Why do you think it is so helpful for us to have someone believe in our abilities?

3 When have you witnessed the power of presence in your life or the life of a loved one? Why is it so important to sit with others in their experiences and to show them that we are there for them?

4 Do you ever feel like you can't do anything useful for the people around you? What scripture passages encourage you in these times? How does prayer help you?

5 Why is it sometimes easy to forget to spend time with God? Name some spiritual practices that help to keep you in God's presence.

Wednesday 28 December

1 What is the most interesting part of creation that you have observed? What does it teach you about both God and creation?

2 In what ways are you encouraged by the fact that God cares for even the smallest parts of creation? How does that knowledge strengthen your faith when you pray or seek God's help?

3 When you begin feeling like a small or unimportant part of the world, what scripture passages remind you that God hears and loves you? When have you witnessed that truth in your own life?

4 As you ponder God's care for every creature in the universe, what thoughts about God come to mind? What is it like to know that you cannot comprehend the magnitude of God's love and care?

5 In what ways do you strive to mirror God's care and love for creation? How do you attempt to show care to everyone and everything you encounter each day?

Journal page

Journal page

Become a Friend of BRF
and give regularly to support our ministry

We help people of all ages to grow in faith

We encourage and support individual Christians and churches as they serve and resource the changing spiritual needs of communities today.

Through **Anna Chaplaincy** we're enabling churches to provide spiritual care to older people

Through **Living Faith** we're nurturing faith and resourcing life-long discipleship

Through **Messy Church** we're helping churches to reach out to families

Through **Parenting for Faith** we're supporting parents as they raise their children in the Christian faith

Our ministry is only possible because of the generous support of individuals, churches, trusts and gifts in wills.

As we look to the future and make plans, **regular donations make a huge difference** in ensuring we can both start and finish projects well.

By becoming a Friend of BRF and giving regularly to our ministry you are partnering with us in the gospel and helping change lives.

How your gift makes a difference

£2 a month — Helps us to develop **Living Faith** resources to use in care homes and communities

£10 a month — Helps us to support churches running the **Parenting for Faith** course and stand alongside parents

£5 a month — Helps us to support **Messy Church** volunteers and resource and grow the wider network

£20 a month — Helps us to resource **Anna Chaplaincy** and improve spiritual care for older people

How to become a Friend of BRF

Set up a Direct Debit donation at **brf.org.uk/donate** or find out how to set up a Standing Order at **brf.org.uk/friends**

Contact the fundraising team

Email: **giving@brf.org.uk**
Tel: +44 (0)1235 462305
Post: Fundraising team, BRF, 15 The Chambers, Vineyard, Abingdon OX14 3FE

Good to know

If you have any questions, or if you want to change your regular donation or stop giving in the future, do get in touch.

Registered with

FR

FUNDRAISING **REGULATOR**

SHARING OUR VISION – MAKING A ONE-OFF GIFT

I would like to make a donation to support BRF.
Please use my gift for:

☐ Where it is most needed ☐ Anna Chaplaincy ☐ Living Faith
☐ Messy Church ☐ Parenting for Faith

Title	First name/initials	Surname

Address

	Postcode

Email

Telephone

Signature	Date

Our ministry is only possible because of the generous support of individuals, churches, trusts and gifts in wills.

giftaid it You can add an extra 25p to every £1 you give.

Please treat as Gift Aid donations all qualifying gifts of money made

☐ today, ☐ in the past four years, ☐ and in the future.

I am a UK taxpayer and understand that if I pay less Income Tax and/or Capital Gains Tax in the current tax year than the amount of Gift Aid claimed on all my donations, it is my responsibility to pay any difference.

☐ My donation does not qualify for Gift Aid.

Please notify BRF if you want to cancel this Gift Aid declaration, change your name or home address, or no longer pay sufficient tax on your income and/or capital gains.

Please complete other side of form ➡

SHARING OUR VISION – MAKING A ONE-OFF GIFT

Please accept my gift of:

☐ £2 ☐ £5 ☐ £10 ☐ £20 Other £ [ ]

by (*delete as appropriate*):

☐ Cheque/Charity Voucher payable to 'BRF'

☐ MasterCard/Visa/Debit card/Charity card

Name on card

Card no. [ ][ ][ ][ ] [ ][ ][ ][ ] [ ][ ][ ][ ] [ ][ ][ ][ ]

Expires end [M][M] [Y][Y]   Security code [ ][ ][ ]   Last 3 digits on the reverse of the card

Signature   Date

☐ I would like to leave a gift to BRF in my will.
Please send me further information.

For help or advice regarding making a gift, please contact
our fundraising team +44 (0)1865 462305

Your privacy

We will use your personal data to process this transaction.
From time to time we may send you information about the
work of BRF that we think may be of interest to you. Our
privacy policy is available at **brf.org.uk/privacy**. Please
contact us if you wish to discuss your mailing preferences.

Registered with

FUNDRAISING
REGULATOR

◖ Please complete other side of form

Please return this form to 'Freepost BRF'
No other address information or stamp is needed

Bible Reading Fellowship is a charity (233280) and company limited by guarantee (301324),
registered in England and Wales

UR0322

In this year's BRF Advent book Sally Welch explores two questions: What is the Christmas story really about, and how do we share it? Through each week of Advent, a different aspect of the Christmas story is examined: light, promise, mystery, love, peace and hope. Within each week, the days are focused on the ways in which the Christmas story is shared: prophecies, journeys, new life, signs, poems, stories and conversations. Each day offers a Bible passage, a reflection and a prayer activity, and suggestions for group study are also included.

Sharing the Christmas Story
From reading to living the gospel
Sally Welch
978 1 80039 106 2 £8.99
brfonline.org.uk

Prayer is at the heart of BRF's work, and this special illustrated anniversary collection is a celebration of prayer for BRF's centenary year. It can be used in a range of different settings, from individual devotions to corporate worship. Including sections on prayers of preparation, seasonal prayers, and themed prayers for special times and hard times, it is the perfect daily companion to resource your spiritual journey.

The BRF Book of 100 Prayers
Resourcing your spiritual journey
Martyn Payne
978 1 80039 147 5 £12.99
brfonline.org.uk

How to encourage Bible reading in your church

BRF has been helping individuals connect with the Bible for 100 years. We want to support churches as they seek to encourage church members into regular Bible reading.

Order a Bible reading resources pack

This pack is designed to give your church the tools to publicise our Bible reading notes. It includes:

- Sample Bible reading notes for your congregation to try.
- Publicity resources, including a poster.
- A church magazine feature about Bible reading notes.

The pack is free, but we welcome a £5 donation to cover the cost of postage. If you require a pack to be sent outside the UK or require a specific number of sample Bible reading notes, please contact us for postage costs. For more information about what the current pack contains, go to **brfonline.org.uk/pages/bible-reading-resources-pack**.

How to order and find out more

- Email **enquiries@brf.org.uk**
- Telephone BRF on +44 (0)1865 319700 Mon–Fri 9.30–17.00
- Write to us at BRF, 15 The Chambers, Vineyard, Abingdon OX14 3FE.

Keep informed about our latest initiatives

We are continuing to develop resources to help churches encourage people into regular Bible reading, wherever they are on their journey. Join our email list at **brfonline.org.uk/signup** to stay informed about the latest initiatives that your church could benefit from.

Subscriptions

The Upper Room is published in January, May and September.

Individual subscriptions
The subscription rate for orders for 4 or fewer copies includes postage and packing:

The Upper Room annual individual subscription £18.30

Group subscriptions
Orders for 5 copies or more, sent to ONE address, are post free:
The Upper Room annual group subscription £14.55

Please do not send payment with order for a group subscription. We will send an invoice with your first order.

Please note that the annual billing period for group subscriptions runs from 1 May to 30 April.

Copies of the notes may also be obtained from Christian bookshops.

Single copies of *The Upper Room* cost £4.85.

Prices valid until 30 April 2023.

Giant print version
The Upper Room is available in giant print for the visually impaired, from:

Torch Trust for the Blind
Torch House
Torch Way
Northampton Road
Market Harborough   Tel: +44 (0)1858 438260
LE16 9HL   **torchtrust.org**

THE UPPER ROOM: INDIVIDUAL/GIFT SUBSCRIPTION FORM

All our Bible reading notes can be ordered online by visiting brfonline.org.uk/subscriptions

☐ I would like to take out a subscription myself (complete your name and address details once)

☐ I would like to give a gift subscription (please provide both names and addresses)

Title .... First name/initials .... Surname ....

Address ....

.... Postcode ....

Telephone .... Email ....

Gift subscription name ....

Gift subscription address ....

.... Postcode ....

Gift message (20 words max. or include your own gift card):

....

....

Please send *The Upper Room* beginning with the January 2023 / May 2023 / September 2023 issue (*delete as appropriate*):

Annual individual subscription ☐ £18.30

Optional donation* to support the work of BRF £ ....

Total enclosed £ .... (cheques should be made payable to 'BRF')

*Please complete and return the Gift Aid declaration on page 159 to make your donation even more valuable to us.

Method of payment

Please charge my MasterCard / Visa with £ ....

Card no. ☐☐☐☐ ☐☐☐☐ ☐☐☐☐ ☐☐☐☐

Expires end ☐☐ ☐☐ Security code ☐☐☐ Last 3 digits on the reverse of the card

THE UPPER ROOM: GROUP SUBSCRIPTION FORM

> **All our Bible reading notes can be ordered online by visiting
> brfonline.org.uk/subscriptions**

☐ Please send me .... copies of *The Upper Room* January 2023 /
May 2023 / September 2023 issue (*delete as appropriate*)

Title .... First name/initials .... Surname ....

Address ....

.... Postcode ....

Telephone .... Email ....

Please do not send payment with this order. We will send an invoice with
your first order.

Christian bookshops: All good Christian bookshops stock BRF publications.
For your nearest stockist, please contact BRF.

Telephone: The BRF office is open Mon–Fri 9.30–17.00. To place your order,
telephone +44 (0)1865 319700.

Online: brfonline.org.uk/group-subscriptions

☐ Please send me a Bible reading resources pack to encourage Bible
reading in my church

Please return this form with the appropriate payment to:
BRF, 15 The Chambers, Vineyard, Abingdon OX14 3FE

For terms and cancellation information, please visit **brfonline.org.uk/terms**.

Bible Reading Fellowship is a charity (233280) and company limited by guarantee (301324),
registered in England and Wales

UR0322

To order

Online: **brfonline.org.uk**
Telephone: +44 (0)1865 319700 Mon–Fri 9.30–17.00

Delivery times within the UK are normally 15 working days. Prices are correct at the time of going to press but may change without prior notice.

Title	Price	Qty	Total
Sharing the Christmas Story (BRF Advent book 2022)	£8.99		
The BRF Book of 100 Prayers	£12.99		

POSTAGE AND PACKING CHARGES			
Order value	UK	Europe	Rest of world
Under £7.00	£2.00		
£7.00–£29.99	£3.00	Available on request	Available on request
£30.00 and over	FREE		

Total value of books	
Postage and packing	
Donation*	
Total for this order	

* Please complete the Gift Aid declaration below

Please complete in BLOCK CAPITALS

Title .... First name/initials .... Surname..

Address..

.... Postcode ....

Acc. No. .... Telephone ....

Email ....

Gift Aid Declaration

giftaid it

Please treat as Gift Aid donations all qualifying gifts of money made

☐ today, ☐ in the past four years, ☐ and in the future **or** ☐ My donation does not qualify for Gift Aid.

I am a UK taxpayer and understand that if I pay less Income Tax and/or Capital Gains Tax in the current tax year than the amount of Gift Aid claimed on all my donations, it is my responsibility to pay any difference.

Please notify BRF if you want to cancel this declaration, change your name or home address, or no longer pay sufficient tax on your income and/or capital gains.

Method of payment

☐ Cheque (made payable to BRF) ☐ MasterCard / Visa

Card no. ☐☐☐☐ ☐☐☐☐ ☐☐☐☐ ☐☐☐☐

Expires end ☐☐ ☐☐   Security code ☐☐☐   Last 3 digits on the reverse of the card

Please return this form to:

BRF, 15 The Chambers, Vineyard, Abingdon OX14 3FE | **enquiries@brf.org.uk**
For terms and cancellation information, please visit **brfonline.org.uk/terms**.

Bible Reading Fellowship is a charity (233280) and company limited by guarantee (301324), registered in England and Wales

Enabling all ages to grow in faith

Anna Chaplaincy

Living Faith

Messy Church

Parenting for Faith

100 years of BRF

2022 is BRF's 100th anniversary! Look out for details of our special new centenary resources, a beautiful centenary rose and an online thanksgiving service that we hope you'll attend. This centenary year we're focusing on sharing the story of BRF, the story of the Bible – and we hope you'll share your stories of faith with us too.

Find out more at **brf.org.uk/centenary**.

To find out more about our work, visit
brf.org.uk

Sharing
the Story
since 1922